ANYONE CAN DRAW

CARTOON[illegible]MS™

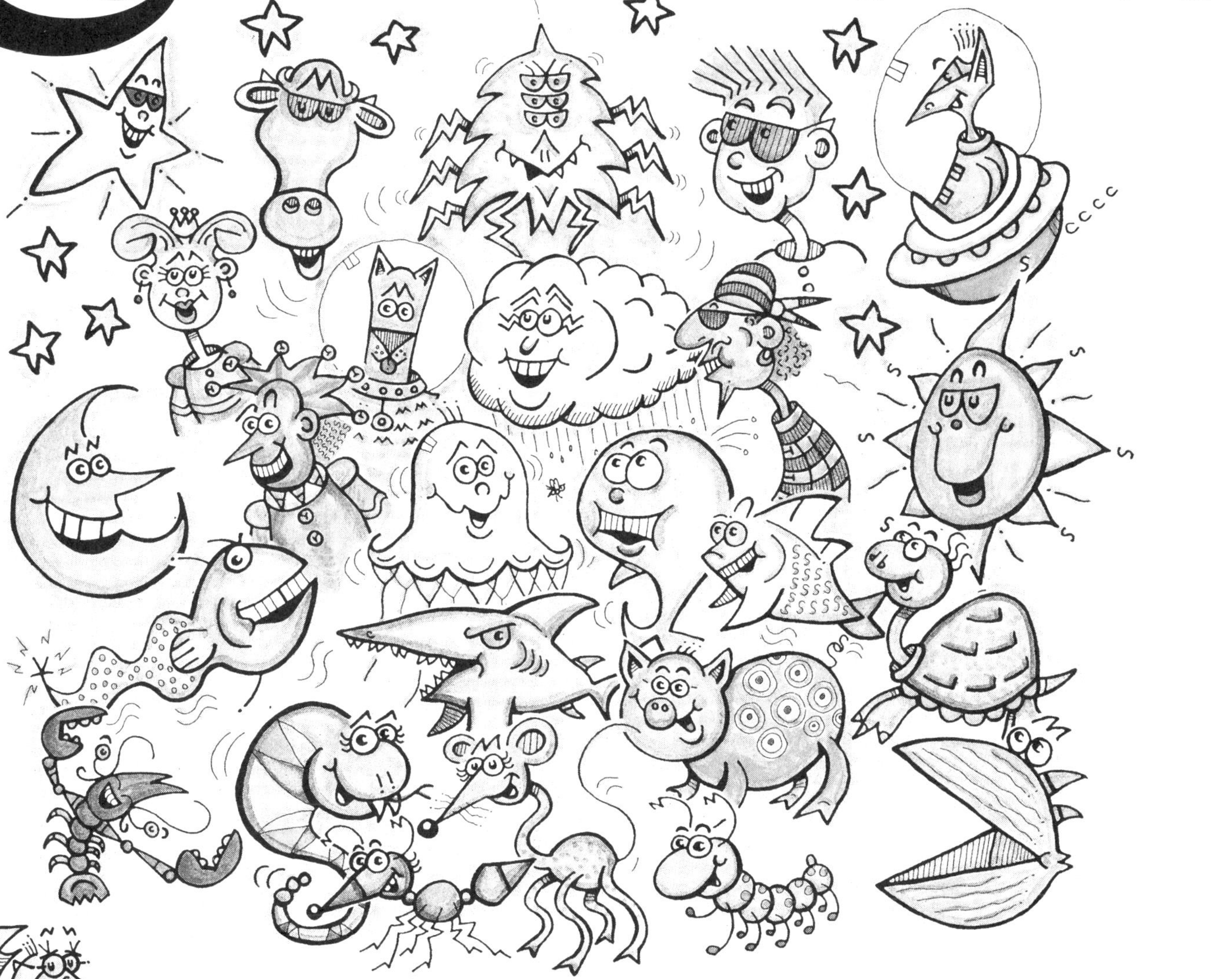

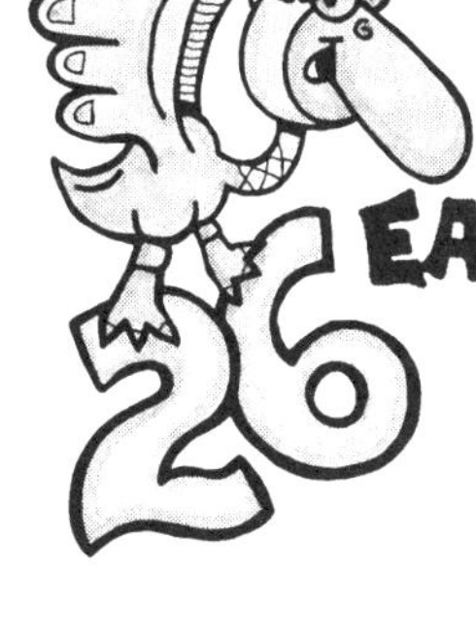

26 EASY TO LEARN, EASY TO REMEMBER CHARACTERS

If you don't believe you can draw,
prepare to believe otherwise.

If you do believe you can draw,
prepare to have even more
fun with your skill…

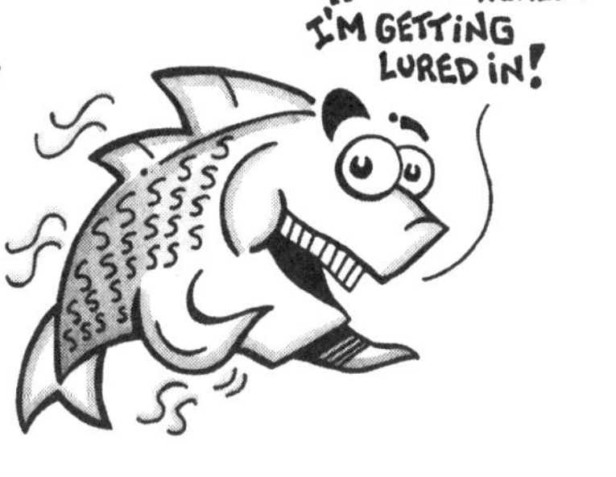

BY STEVE BROSNIHAN EDITED BY RICHARD GOLDMAN

With immense gratitude, I dedicate this book to family and friends who have supported and encouraged me throughout my career, and to the children who have inspired me to create an easy way to share my love of drawing cartoons.

for my mother

A portion of the proceeds from this book is being donated to

The TOMORROW FUND for children with cancer

www.tomorrowfund.org

Fly By Knight Designs
P.O. Box 111
Bristol, RI 02809
(401) 253-5909
www.cartoonagrams.com

ISBN 978-0-9821548-0-9

Printed in the United States of America

First Edition: October 2008
10 9 8 7 6 5 4

STABLE OF CONTENTS

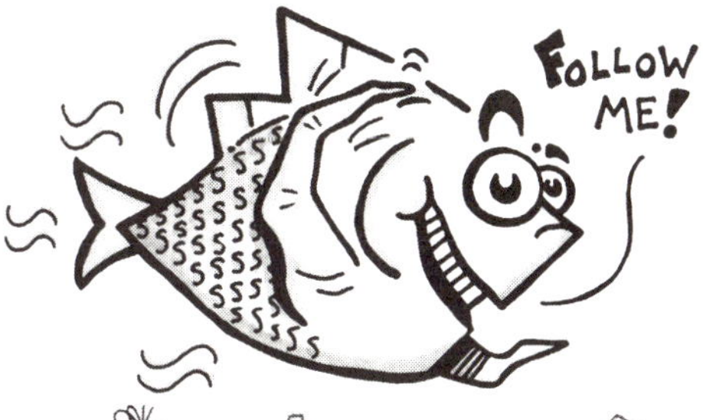

INTRODUCTION

DEAR READER,

Welcome to the first book of **Cartoonagrams™**, cartoons that **Anyone Can Draw**. All you need is: A) the ability to write the letters of the alphabet; B) something to draw with; and C) something to draw on. With those bases covered, you'll soon discover your inner cartoonist.

When I ask kids whether or not they think they can draw cartoons, I often hear answers like "I can't, but my brother can." Too often there is a belief that only one child in a family is predestined to be *the* musician, *the* athlete, or *the* artist.

I love proving to kids, and students of all ages, that Anyone Can Draw and have a blast doing it. With Cartoonagrams™, I can prove this in just a few minutes. The results often inspire a reaction I love hearing: "Wow! I CAN draw! Let's do another one!"

I began creating Cartoonagrams™ while drawing with hospitalized children. Using only the 26 letters of the alphabet, I was able to get kids to draw with confidence by using shapes they knew well. Cartoonagrams™ have proven very easy to learn, as step by step, each letter adds an actual piece to the finished drawing. They're also very easy to remember, thanks to the hint word or phrase that contains all of the letters needed to draw a character.

The Cartoonagrams™ method may be regarded as a *trick* approach to drawing. I'm fine with that. Trick or not, Cartoonagrams™ help reveal creative potential that students might not discover otherwise. They provide a great vehicle for one's imagination that's easy and fun to drive.

ENJOY!,

Steve B.

GUIDELINES

A few guidelines are helpful when drawing Cartoonagrams™…

▶ The 26 letters of the alphabet are the building blocks of Cartoonagrams™. All but one letter is used capitalized. The exception is the letter "i" — it is used in lower case because its dot comes in handy.

▶ Only the letters in the hint word or words are used for a specific Cartoonagram™. It is a good idea to mark each letter after the first time you use it. This will help you keep track of letters you still need to use.

▶ Each letter from the hint must be used at least once, and any letter can be used more than once. Hints with multiples of the same letter must use each multiple at least once.

▶ Letters may be drawn in any direction — even upside-down or backwards.

TIPS

C's and **U**'s used for the eyes of Cartoonagrams™ should always be drawn thicker or heavier than usual. This helps the eyes look open and shiny.

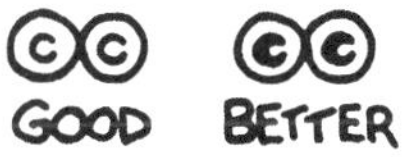

E's are often used for shading. When they are used in this way, it is best to draw them lighter to enhance the shading effect.

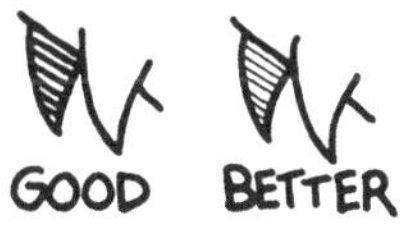

Be sure to start Cartoonagrams™ on your paper where the directions indicate. If you begin a character in the wrong part of your paper, you may run out of room when it comes to finishing it. Make note of whether the character will fit best using the paper the "tall way" or the "long way."

Consider drawing with a marker or crayon to get past the tendency to erase. Erasing may lead to a more perfect drawing in the end, but Cartoonagrams™ truly have more personality when they are imperfect. Always make your best effort, but don't get bogged down by perfectionism.

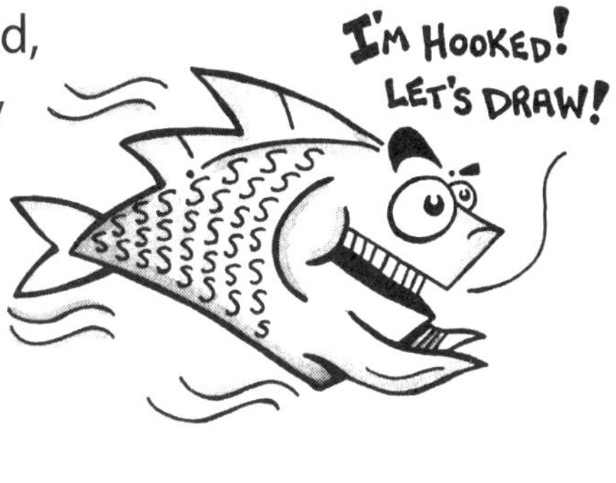

Most importantly: **HAVE FUN** while you learn to draw!

THE CLOVEN MOON

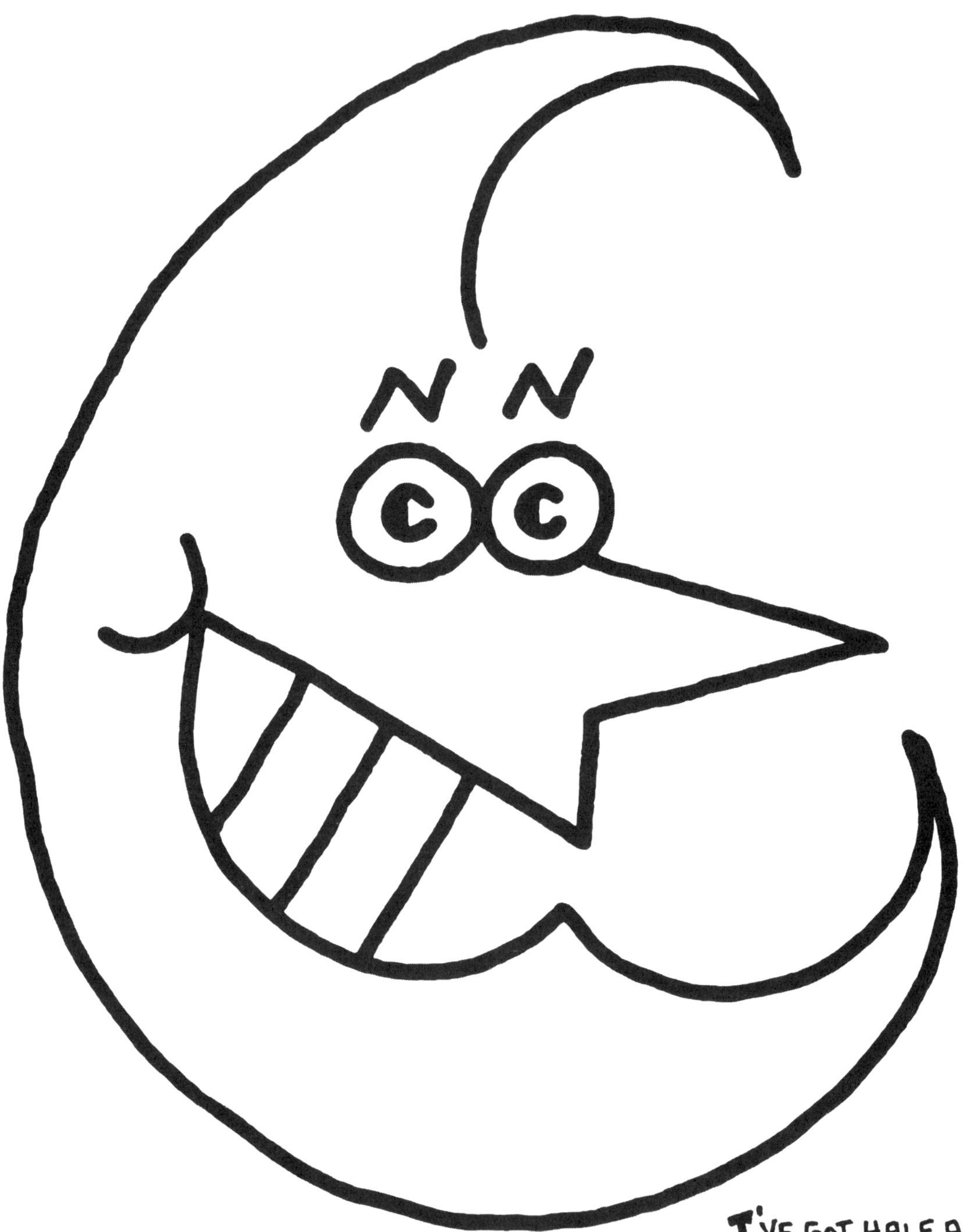

The word **CLOVEN** can be defined as meaning "split in half." That's appropriate since this key word will help you draw a half moon with a smiling face. This cartoonagram is almost like a magic trick because only the final step reveals the identity of the character.

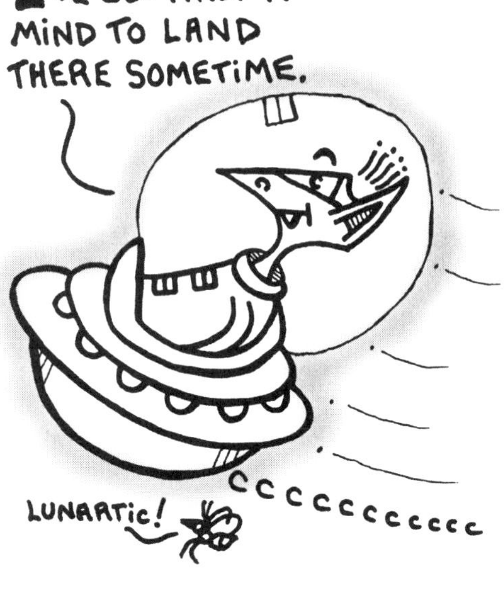

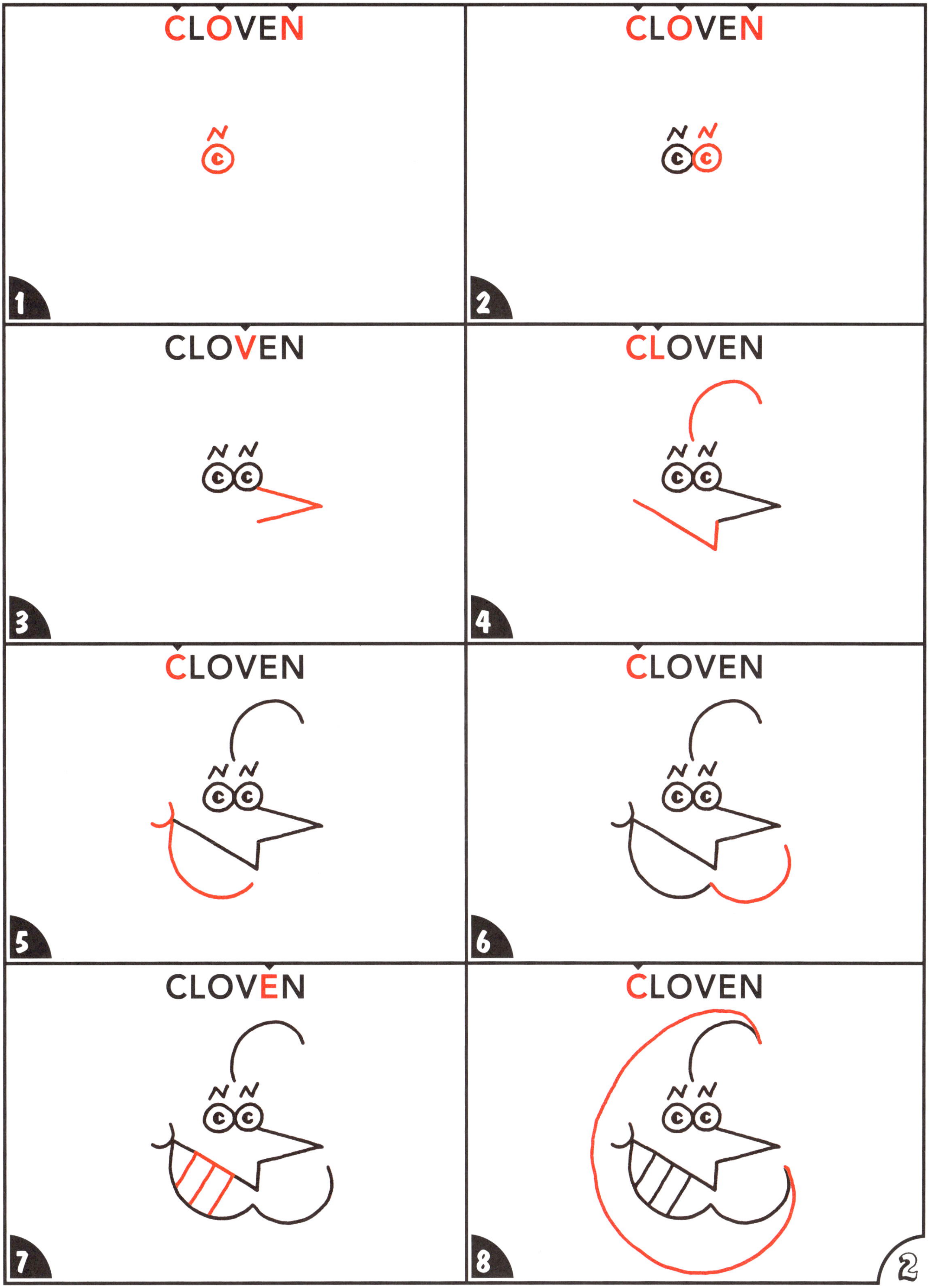
CLOVEN
1
CLOVEN
2
CLOVEN
3
CLOVEN
4
CLOVEN
5
CLOVEN
6
CLOVEN
7
CLOVEN
8

THE OBViOUS SUN

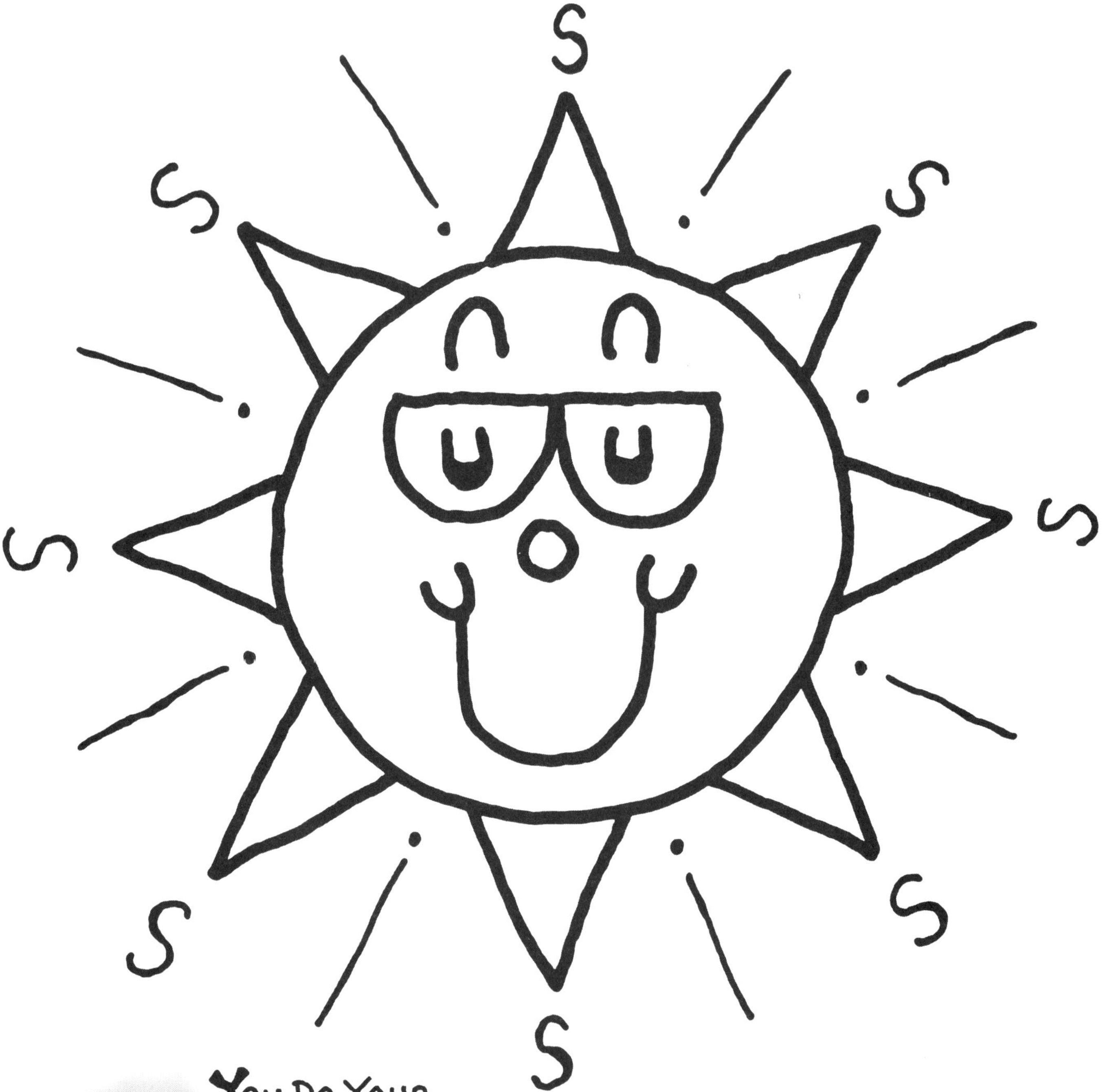

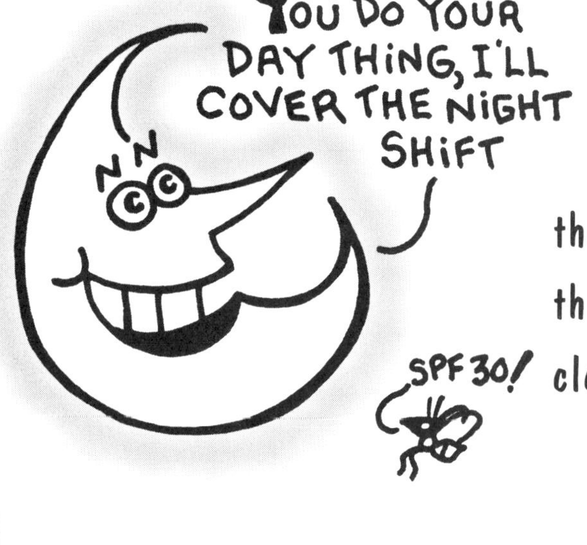

The word **OBViOUS** can be defined as something that is "very clear." You can remember how to draw this cartoonagram by reminding yourself that on a clear day, it's **OBViOUS** the sun is shining.

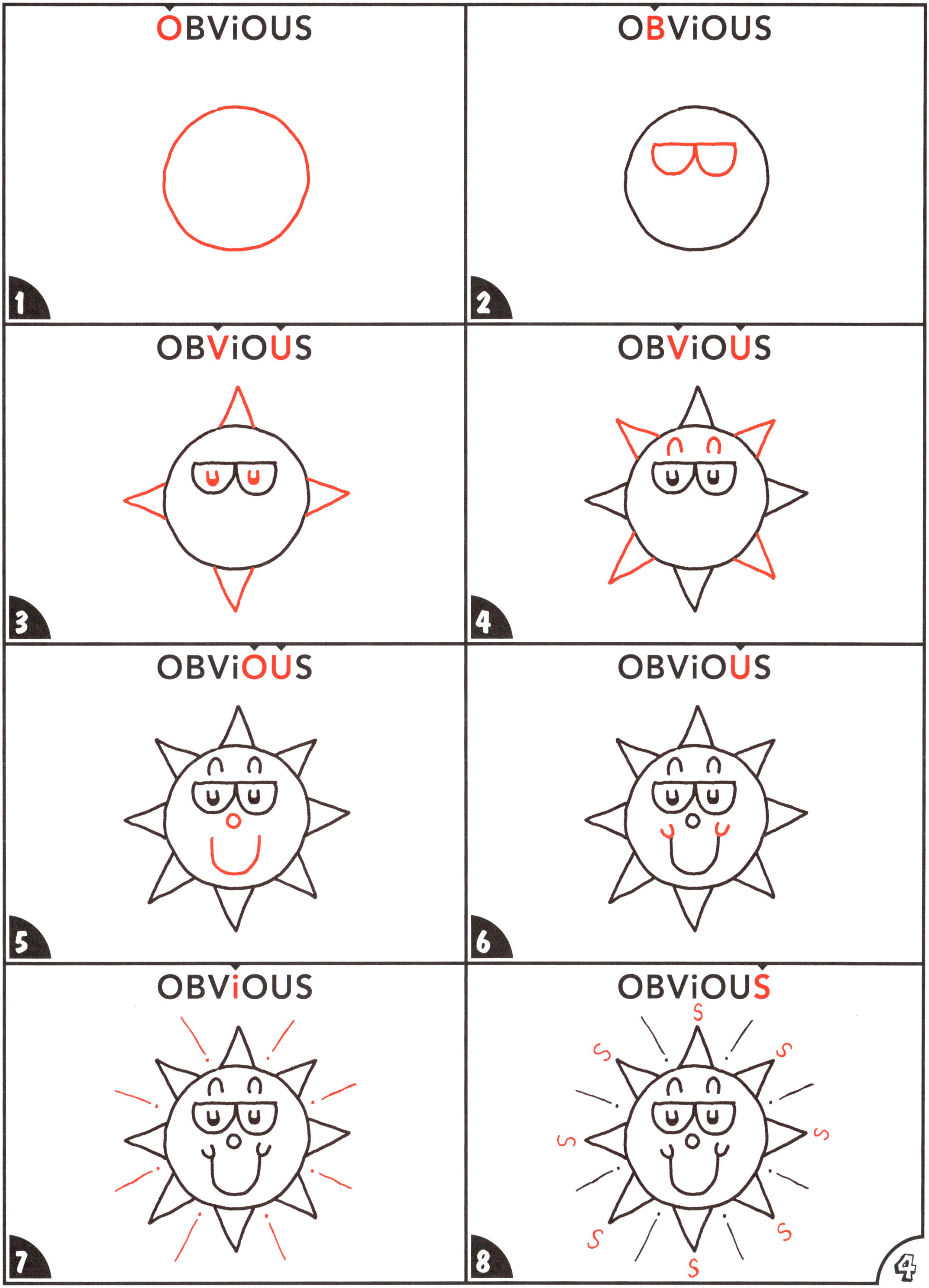
OBViOUS
1
OBViOUS
2
OBViOUS
3
OBViOUS
4
OBViOUS
5
OBViOUS
6
OBViOUS
7
OBViOUS
8

THE i AM iCE STAR

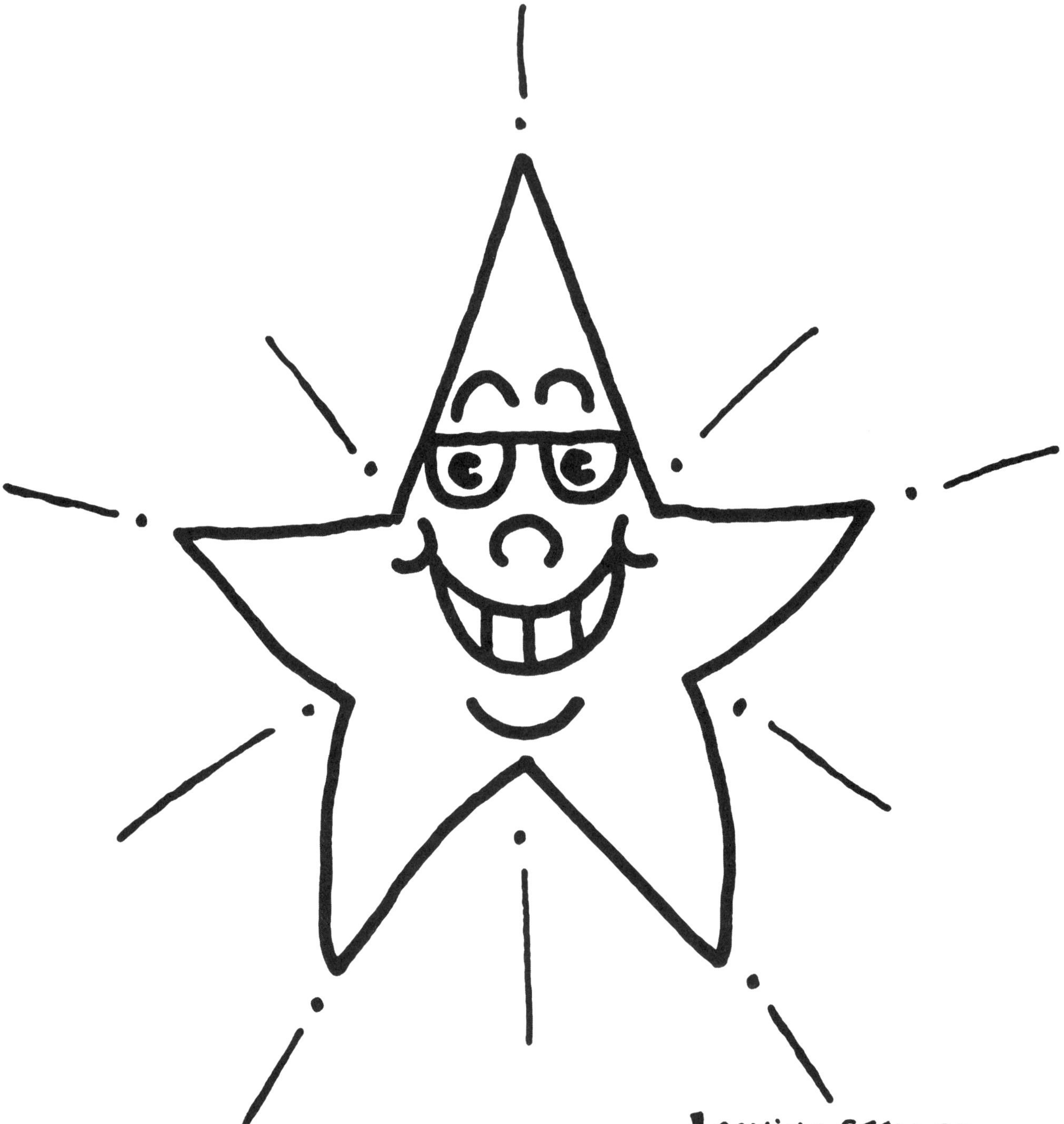

Imagine a star located so far out on the edge of the galaxy that it produces light and energy from the intense cold. If this star could beam a message to us, "**i AM iCE**" is what it would say.

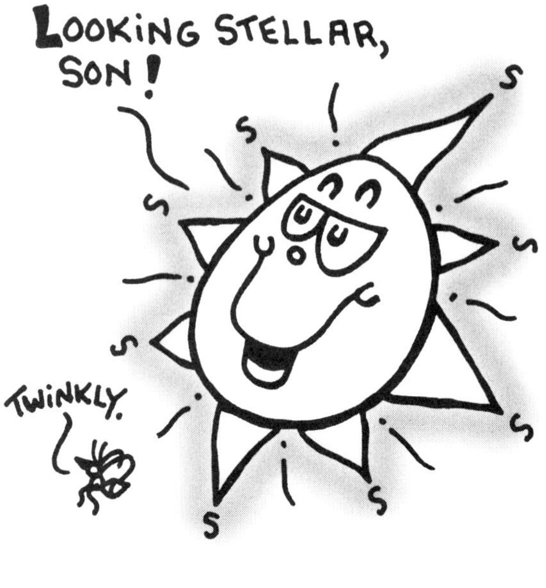

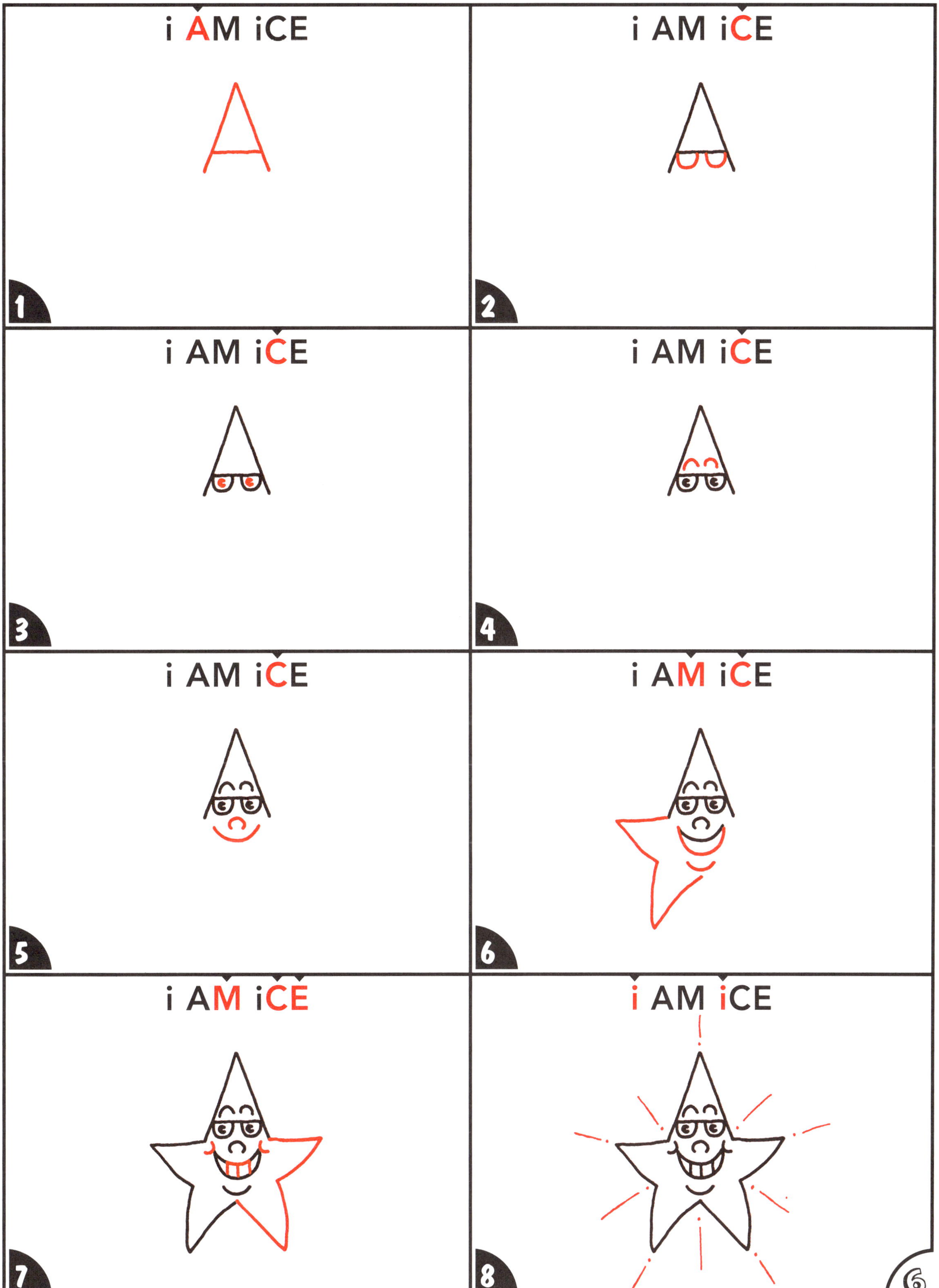
i AM iCE
1
i AM iCE
2
i AM iCE
3
i AM iCE
4
i AM iCE
5
i AM iCE
6
i AM iCE
7
i AM iCE
8

THE SLiMY COiLS SNAKE

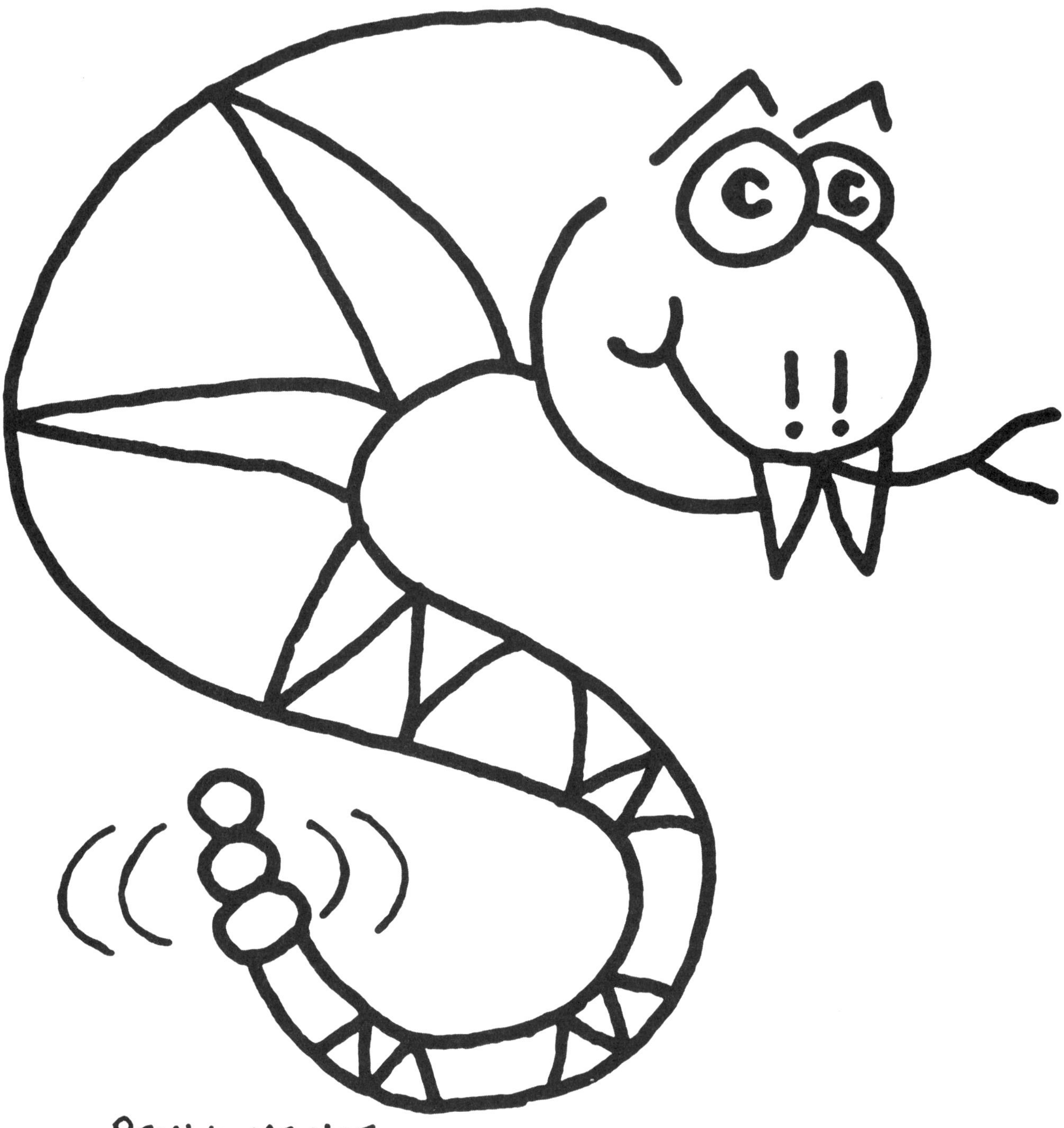

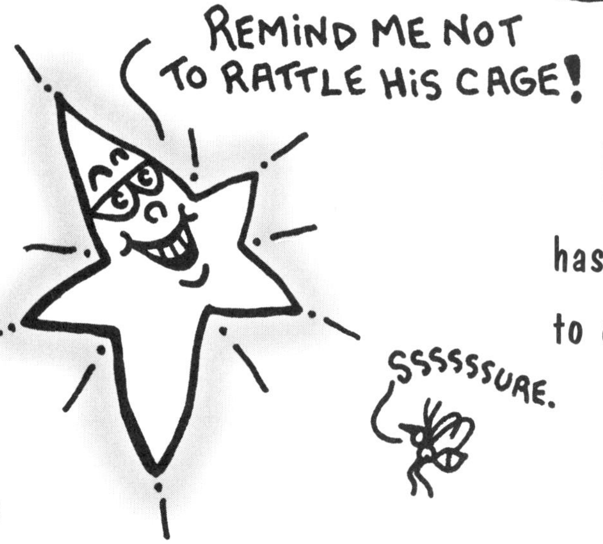

Living in a swamp, this rattling snake sometimes has to wrap itself in **COiLS** around a tree branch to dry out when it gets **SLiMY**.

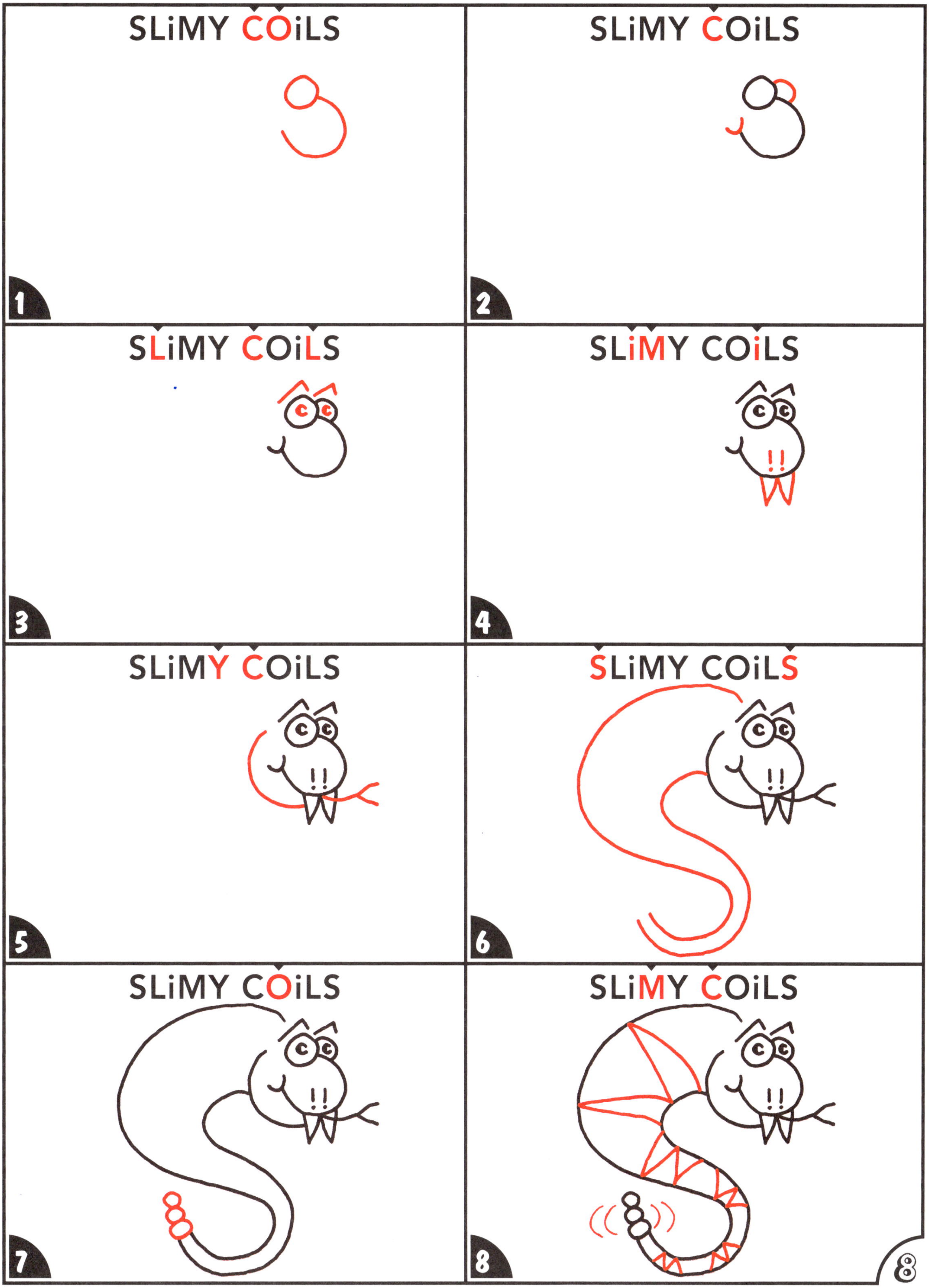
SLiMY COiLS
1
SLiMY COiLS
2
SLiMY COiLS
3
SLiMY COiLS
4
SLiMY COiLS
5
SLiMY COiLS
6
SLiMY COiLS
7
SLiMY COiLS
8

THE COCOON CATERPiLLAR

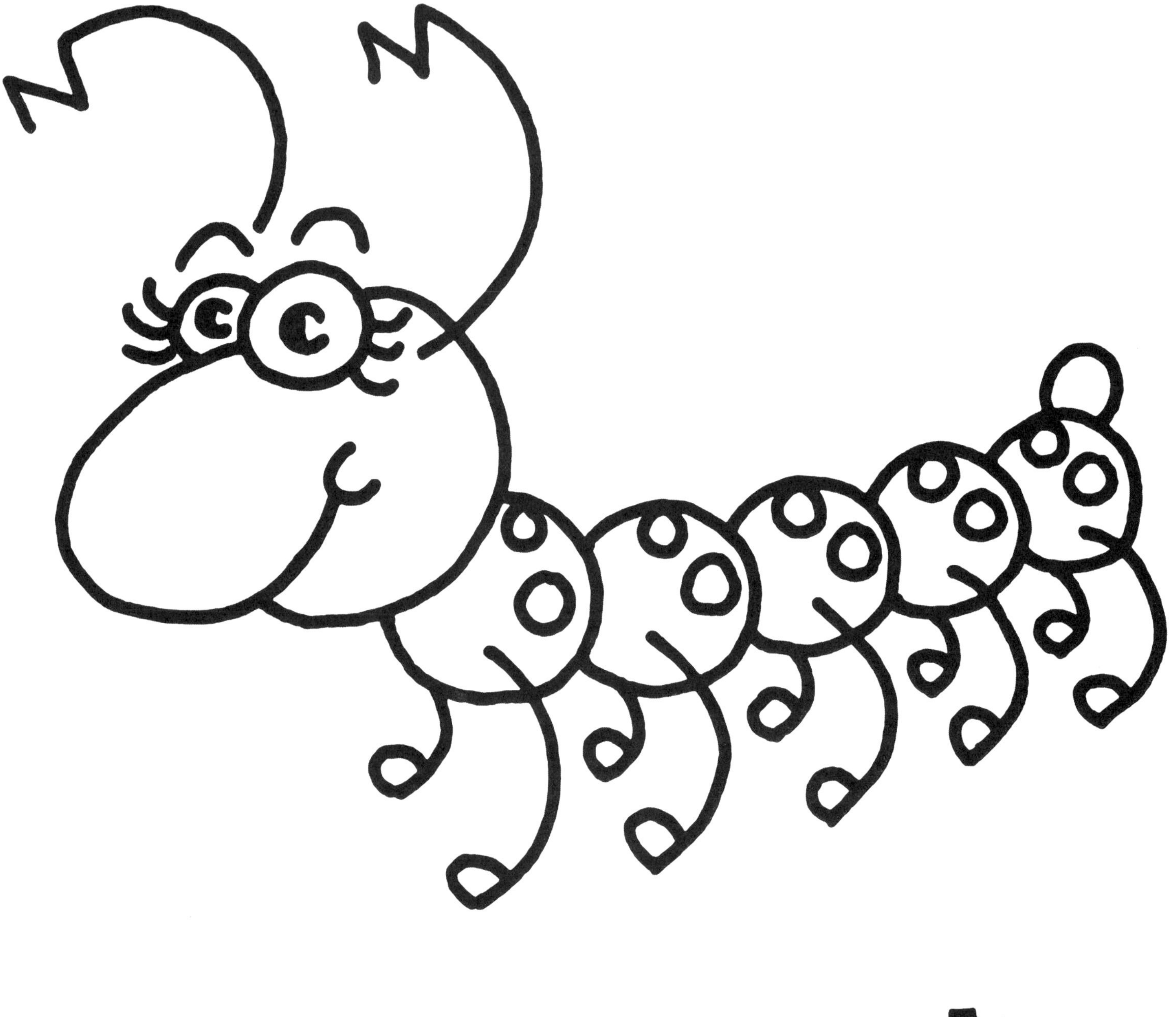

This caterpillar is looking forward to spinning a **COCOON** sometime soon, giving it a chance to show its true colors as a butterfly — or maybe a moth (it's tough to predict).

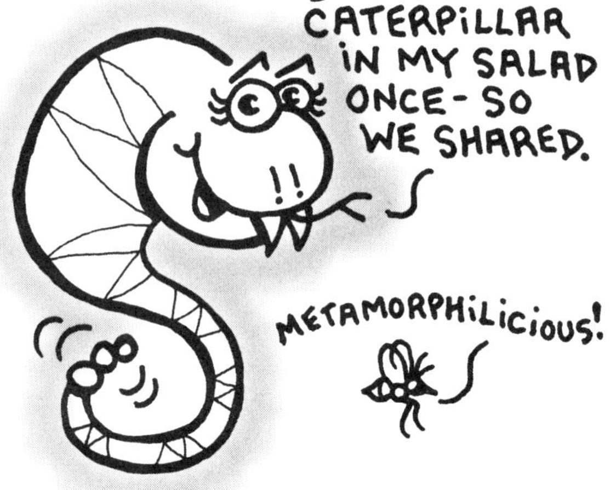

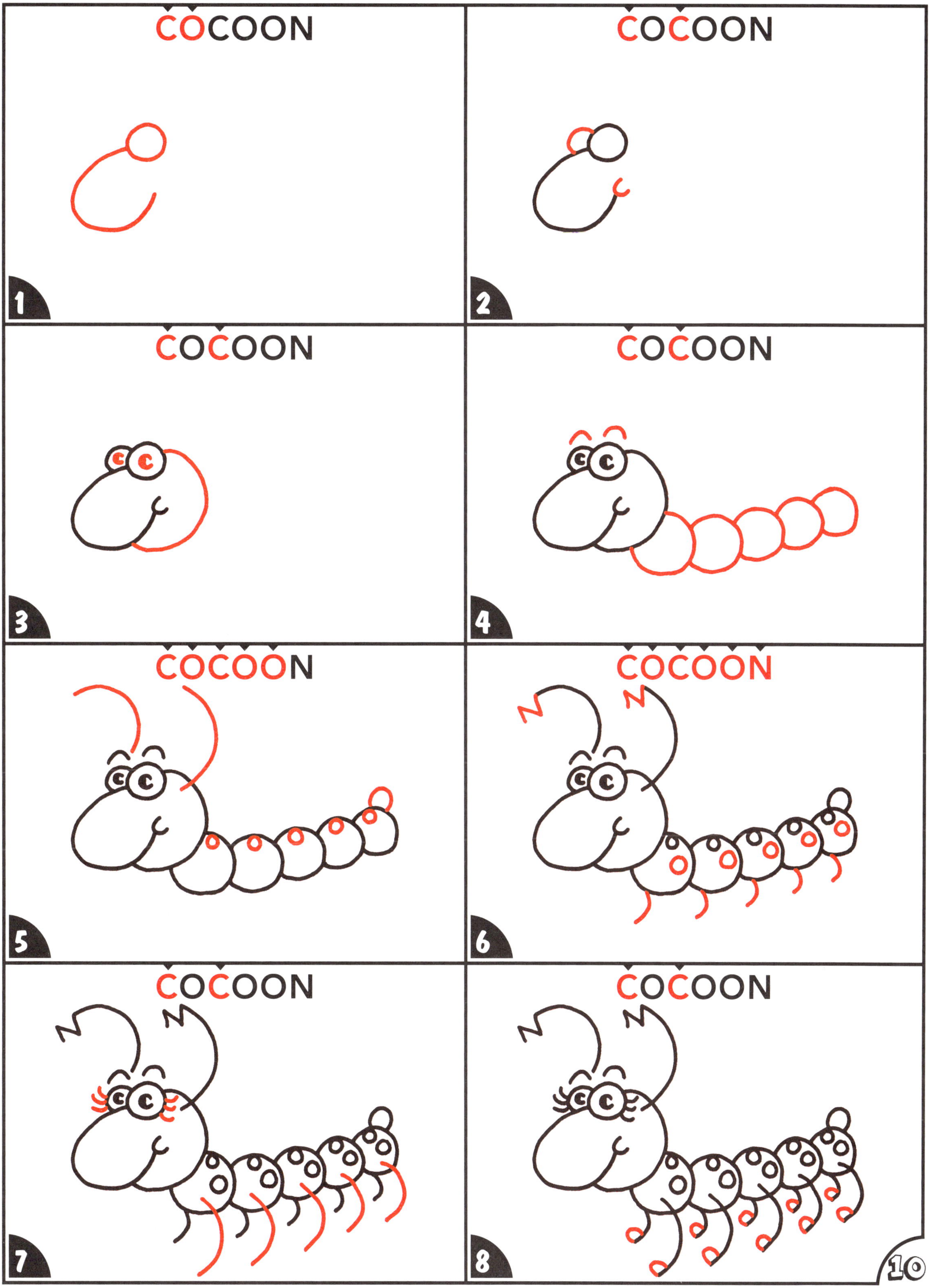
COCOON
1
COCOON
2
COCOON
3
COCOON
4
COCOON
5
COCOON
6
COCOON
7
COCOON
8

THE CLAM MOVIE CLAM

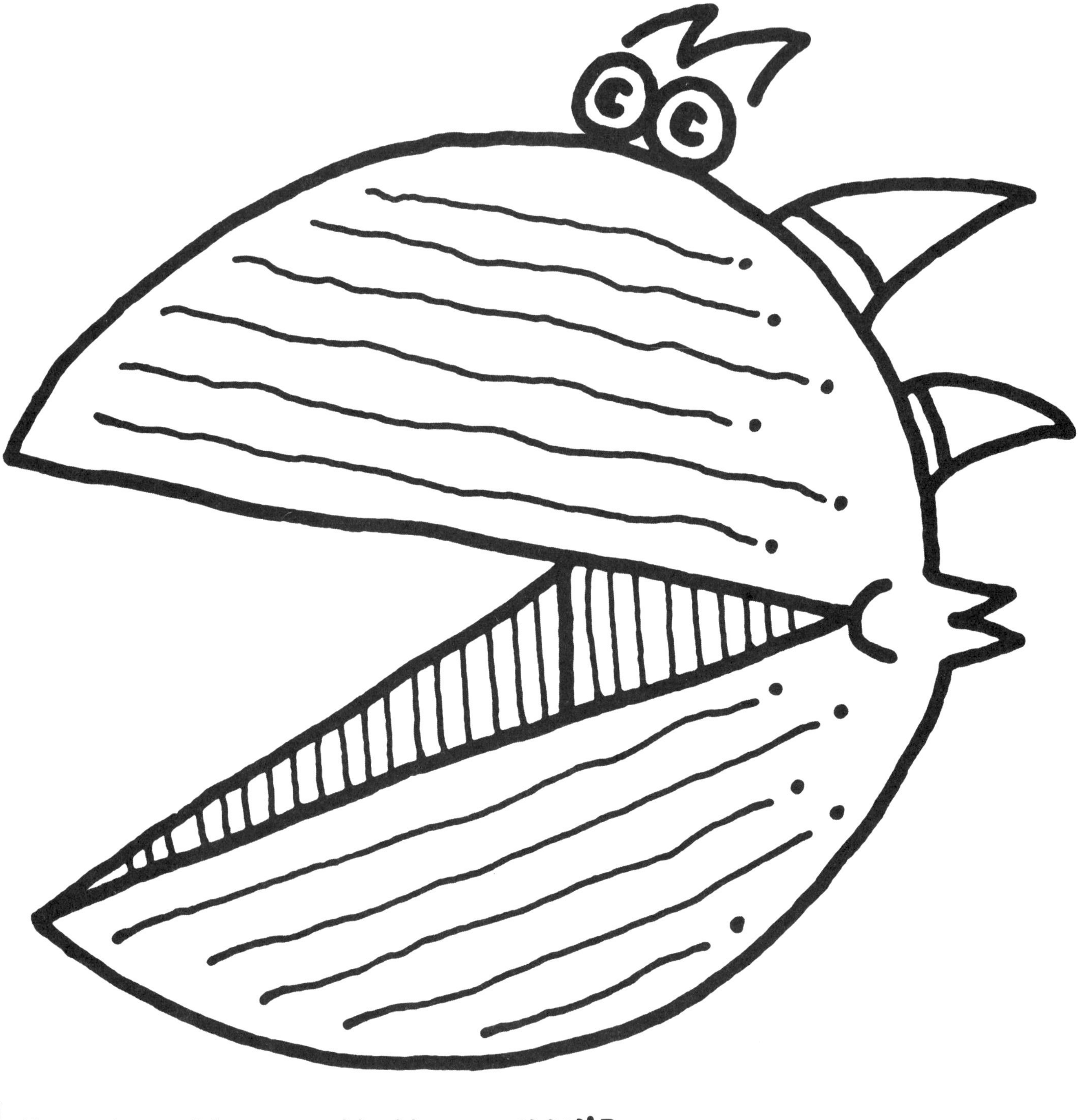

Hollywood is filming a blockbuster **MOViE** about a giant razor-backed **CLAM**. Here's a look at the star of this future box office smash.

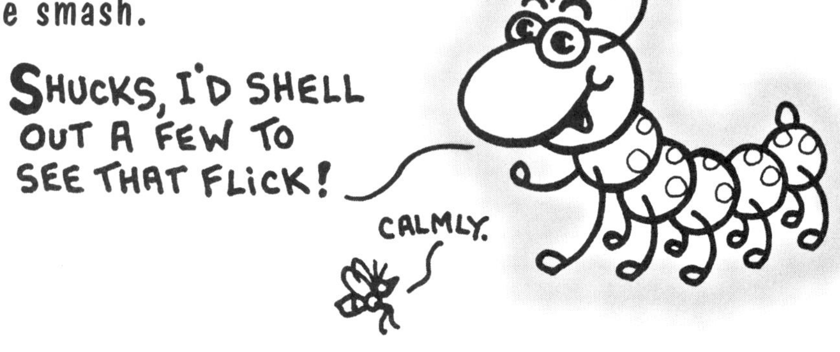

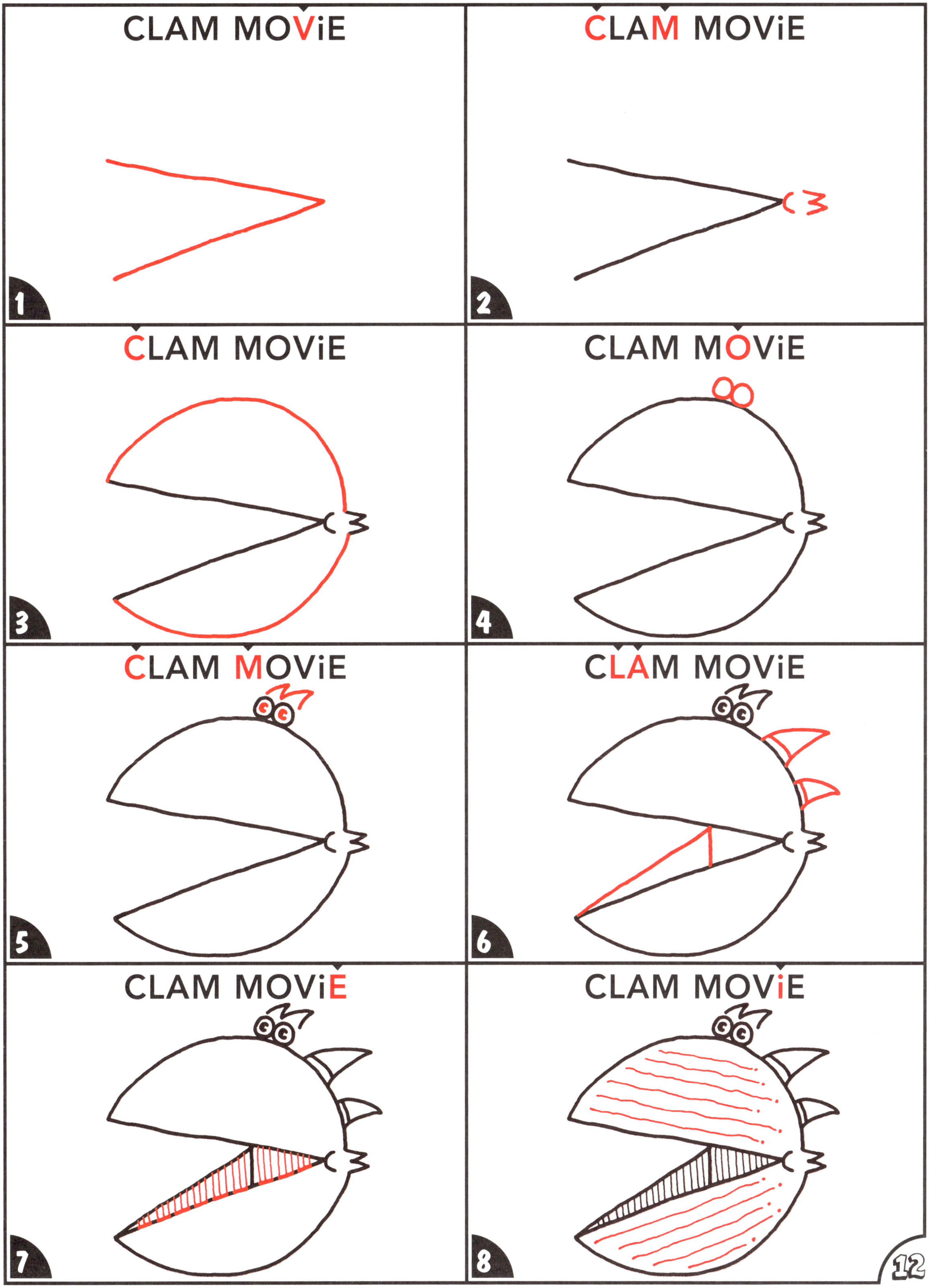
CLAM MOViE
1
CLAM MOViE
2
CLAM MOViE
3
CLAM MOViE
4
CLAM MOViE
5
CLAM MOViE
6
CLAM MOViE
7
CLAM MOViE
8

THE FiSH LOVE MUSiC FiSH

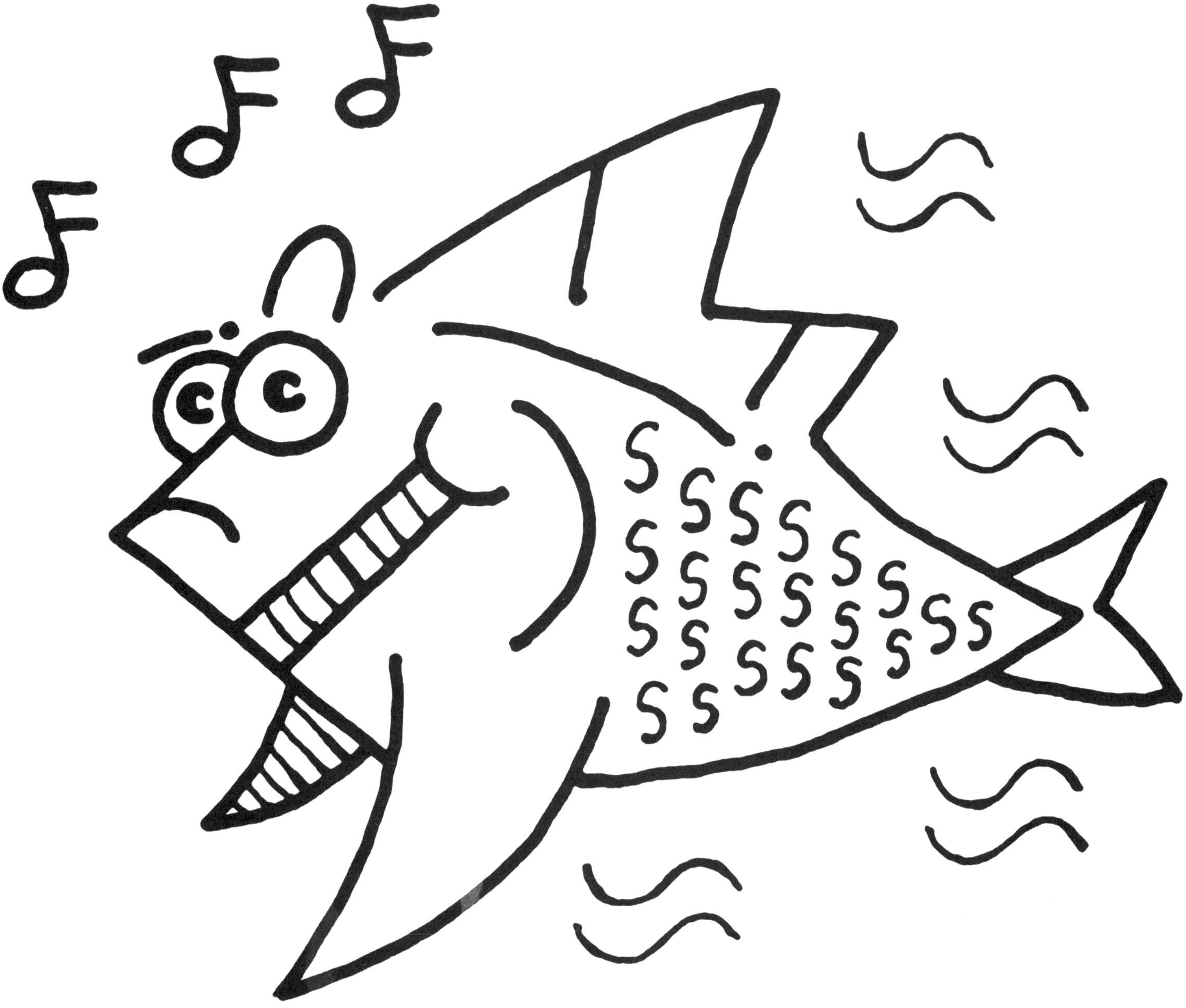

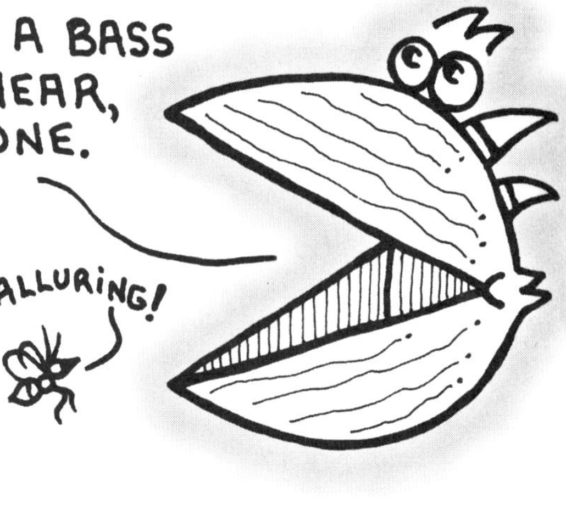

This **FiSH LOVE**s to keep rhythm in its swimming strokes by listening to Finnish sole **MUSiC**. An aspiring singer, it can often be overheard practicing its scales.

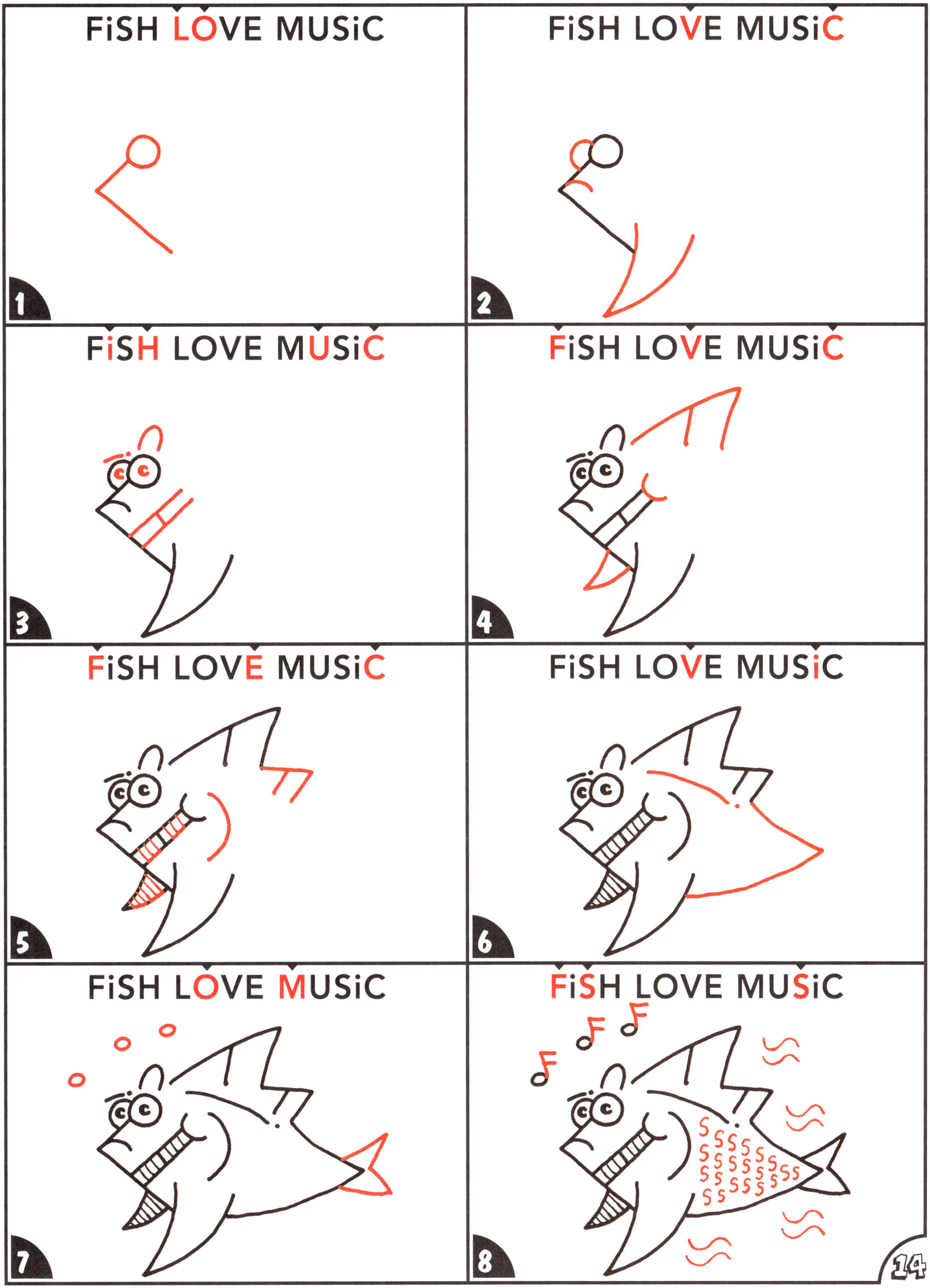
FiSH LOVE MUSiC
1
FiSH LOVE MUSiC
2
FiSH LOVE MUSiC
3
FiSH LOVE MUSiC
4
FiSH LOVE MUSiC
5
FiSH LOVE MUSiC
6
FiSH LOVE MUSiC
7
FiSH LOVE MUSiC
8

THE CLOWN ANT ANT

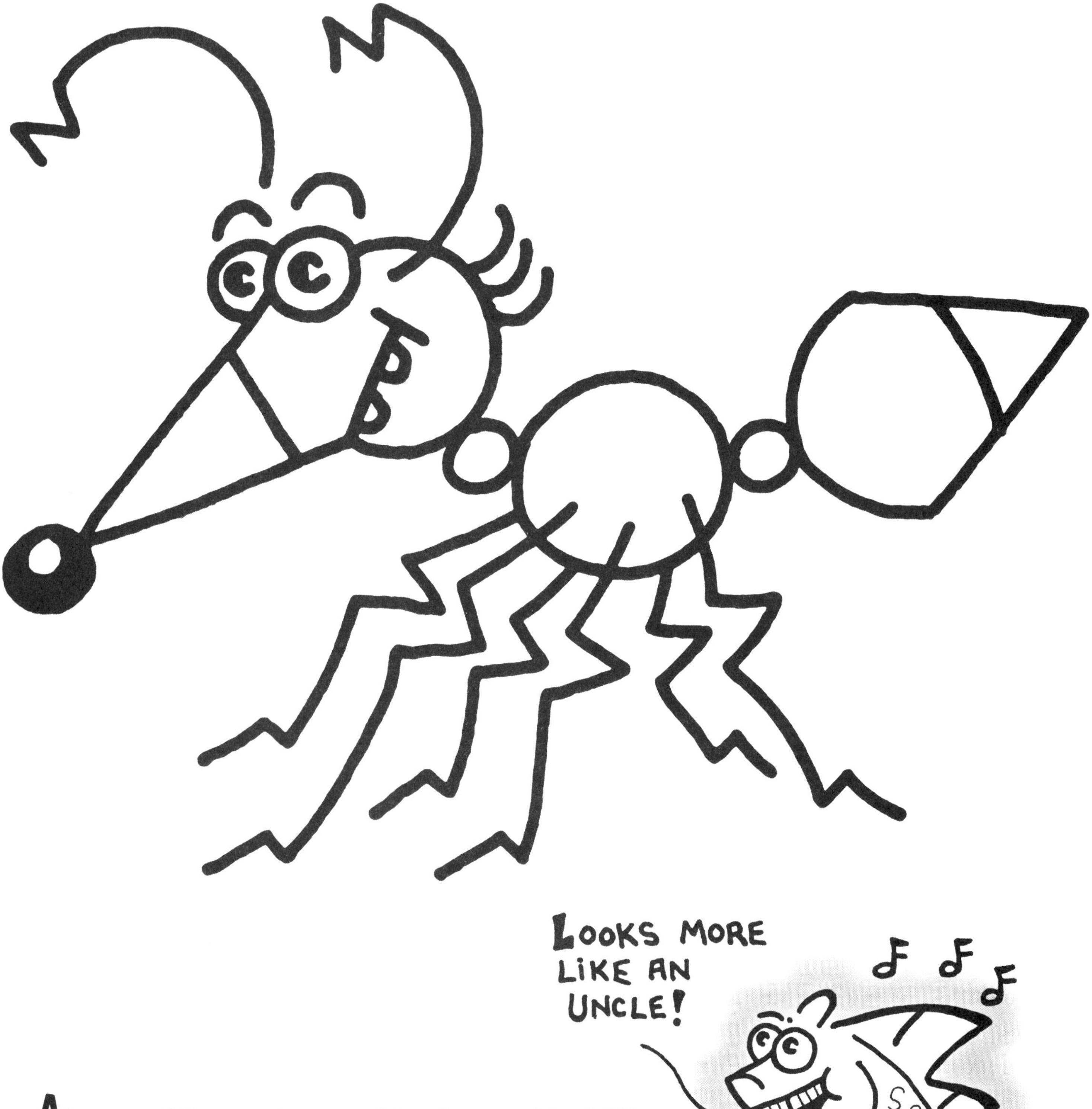

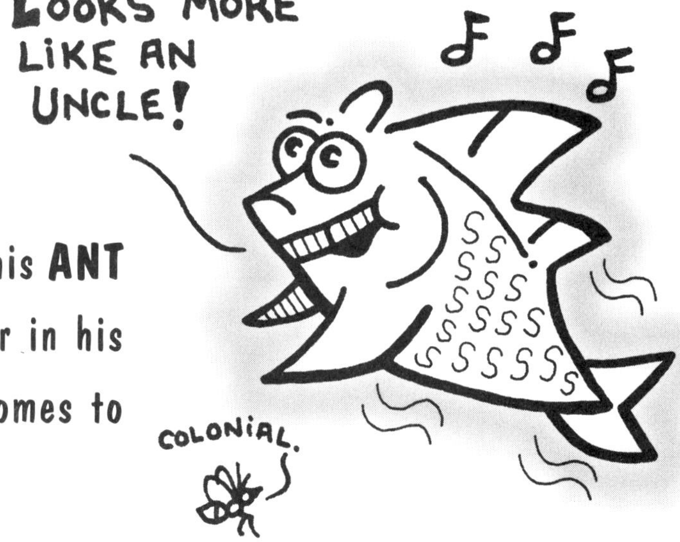

Always willing to do something funny, this **ANT** loves to **CLOWN** around, inspiring laughter in his friends and (very large) family. When it comes to getting giggles, he's king of the hill.

CLOWN ANT

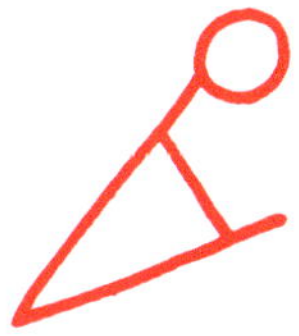

1

CLOWN ANT

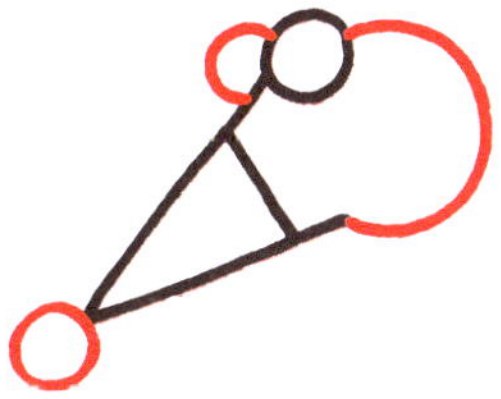

2

CLOWN ANT

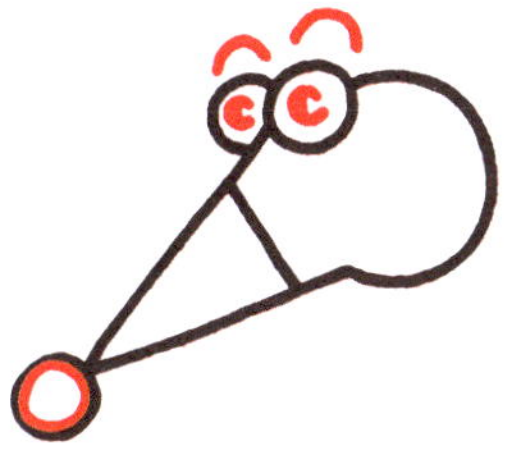

3

CLOWN ANT

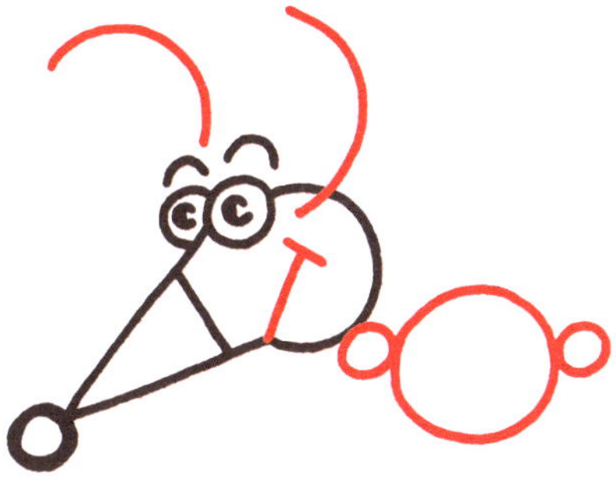

4

CLOWN ANT

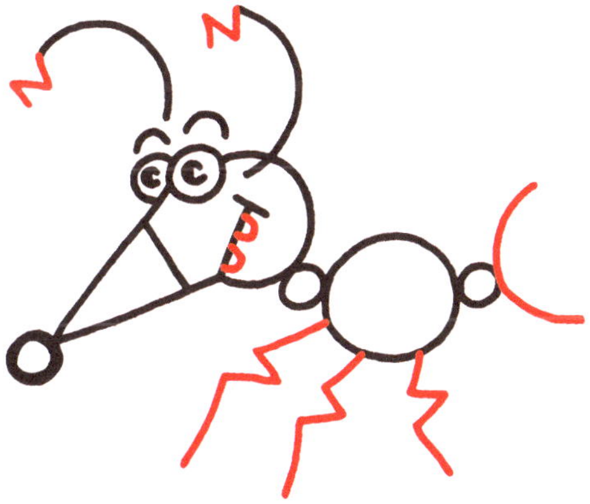

5

CLOWN ANT

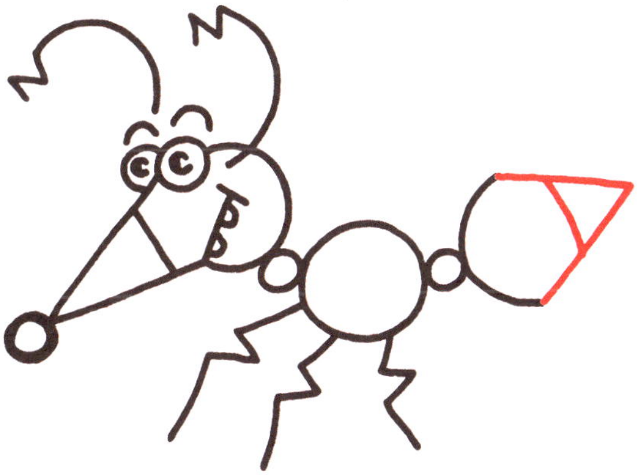

6

CLOWN ANT

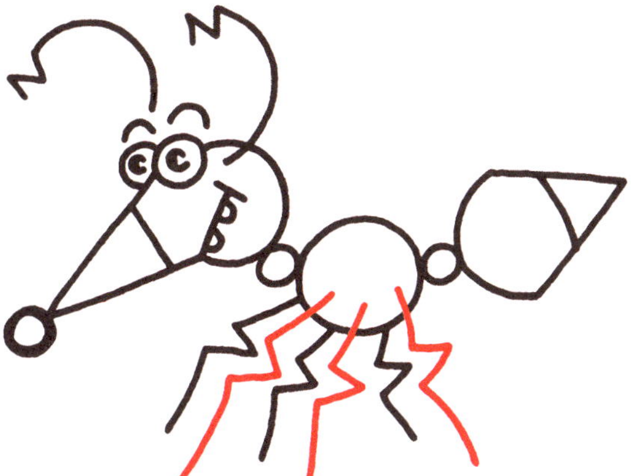

7

CLOWN ANT

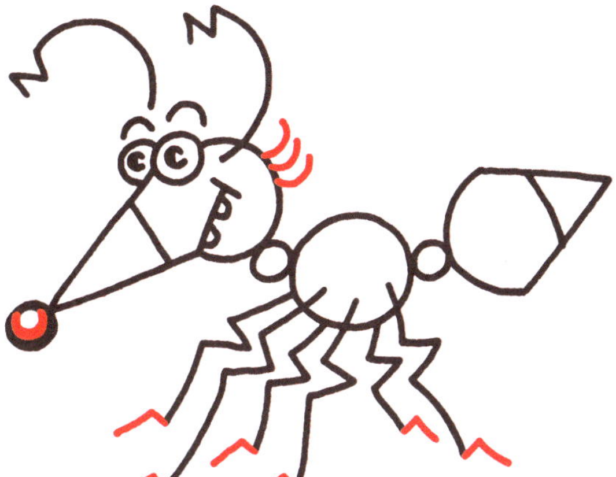

8

THE BLUES COW cow

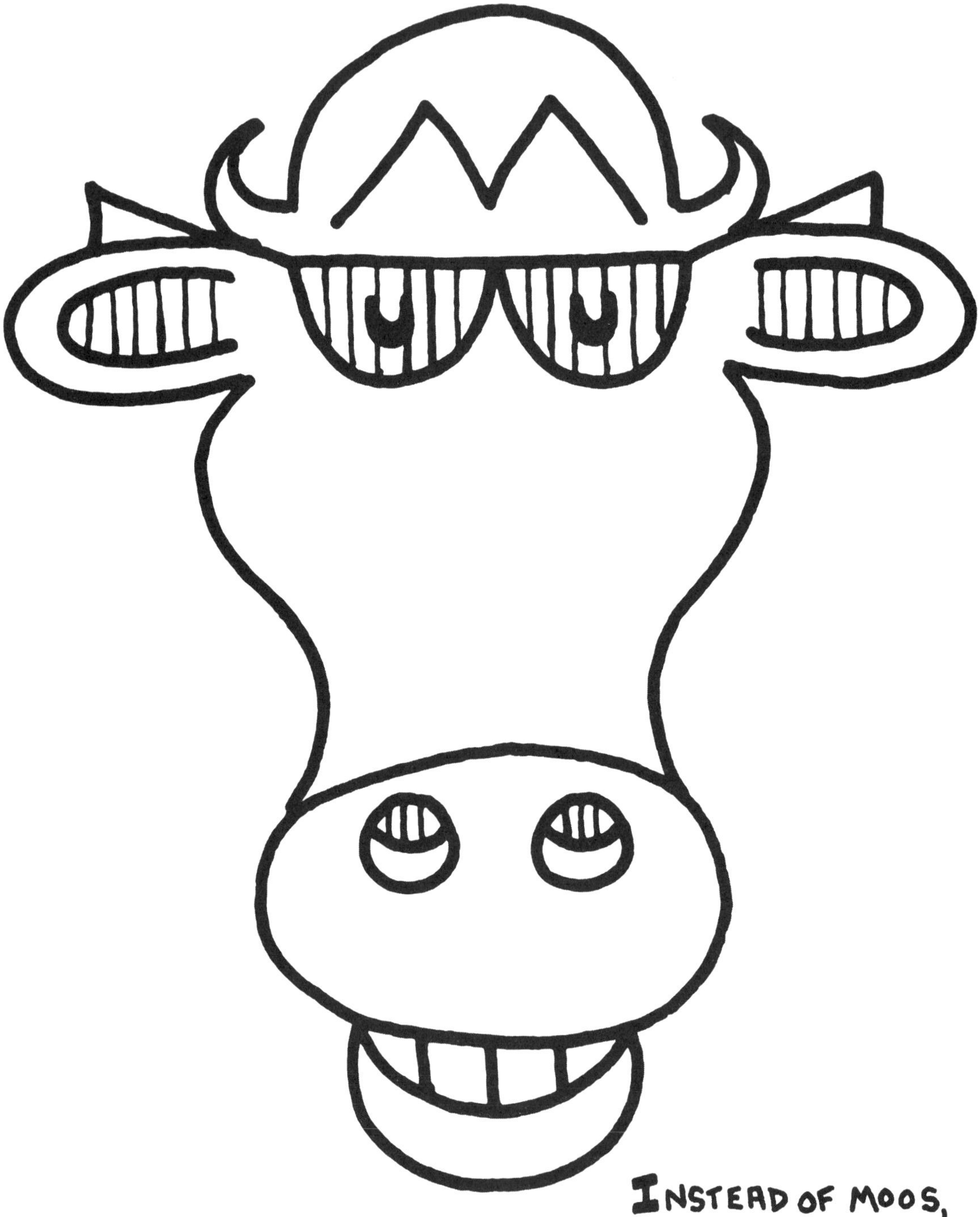

Very hip and very cool, this shades-wearing **COW** can smile about achieving a successful career while singing the **BLUES**. Look forward to her upcoming collaboration with another barnyard vocalist, the SOW's VOiCE pig.

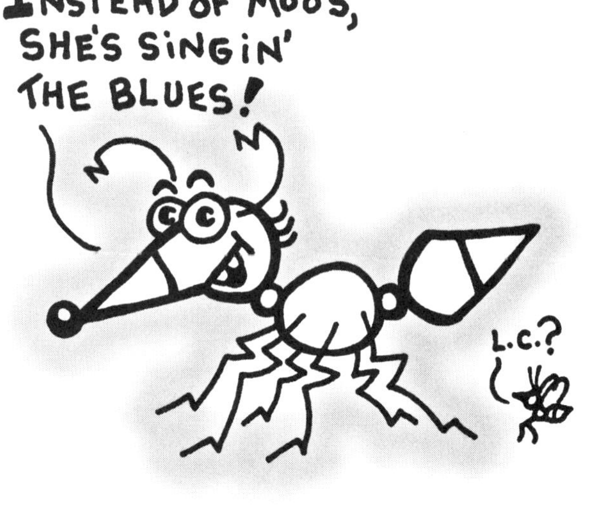

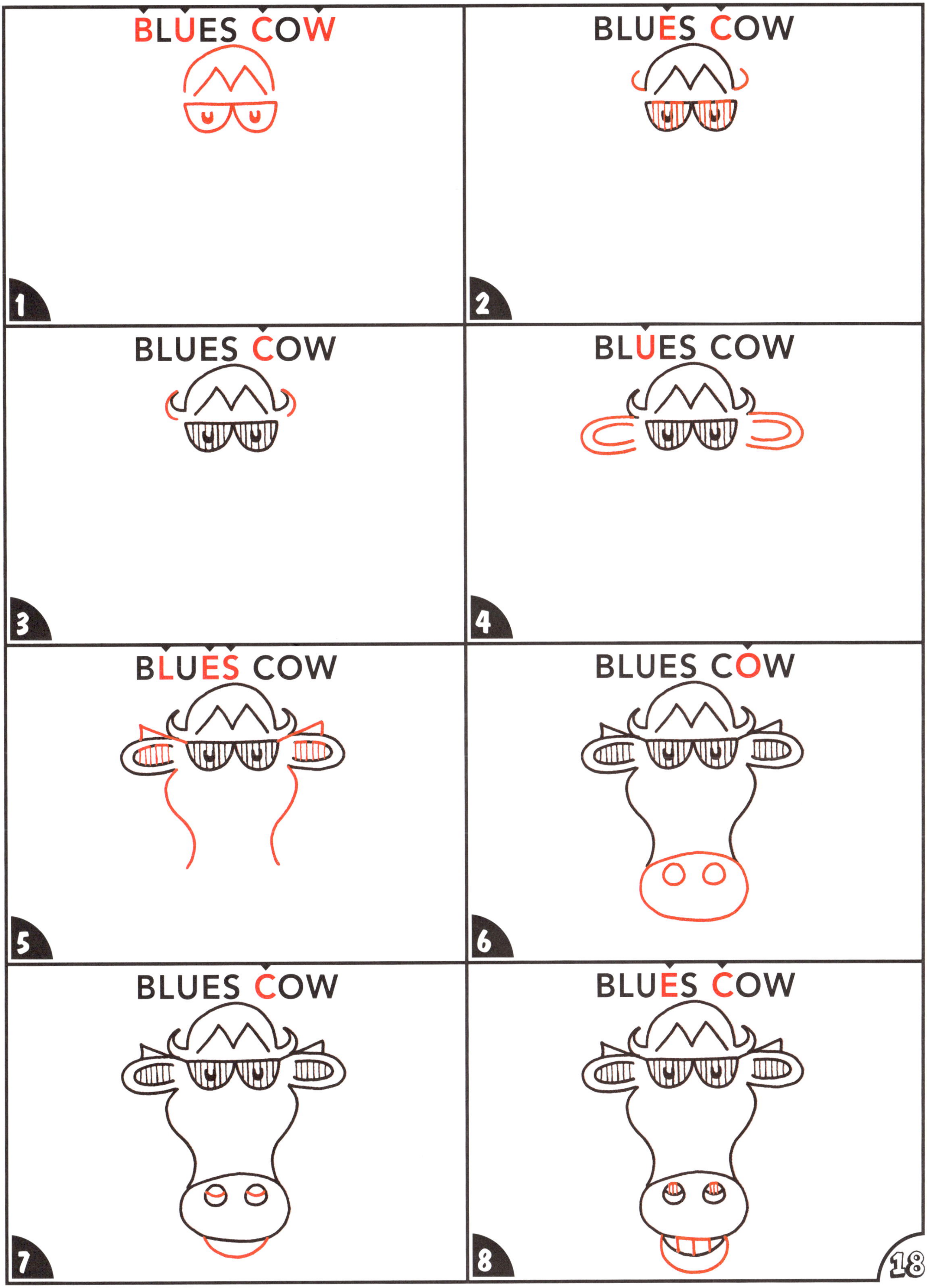
BLUES COW
1
BLUES COW
2
BLUES COW
3
BLUES COW
4
BLUES COW
5
BLUES COW
6
BLUES COW
7
BLUES COW
8

THE WHALE'S VOiCE WHALE

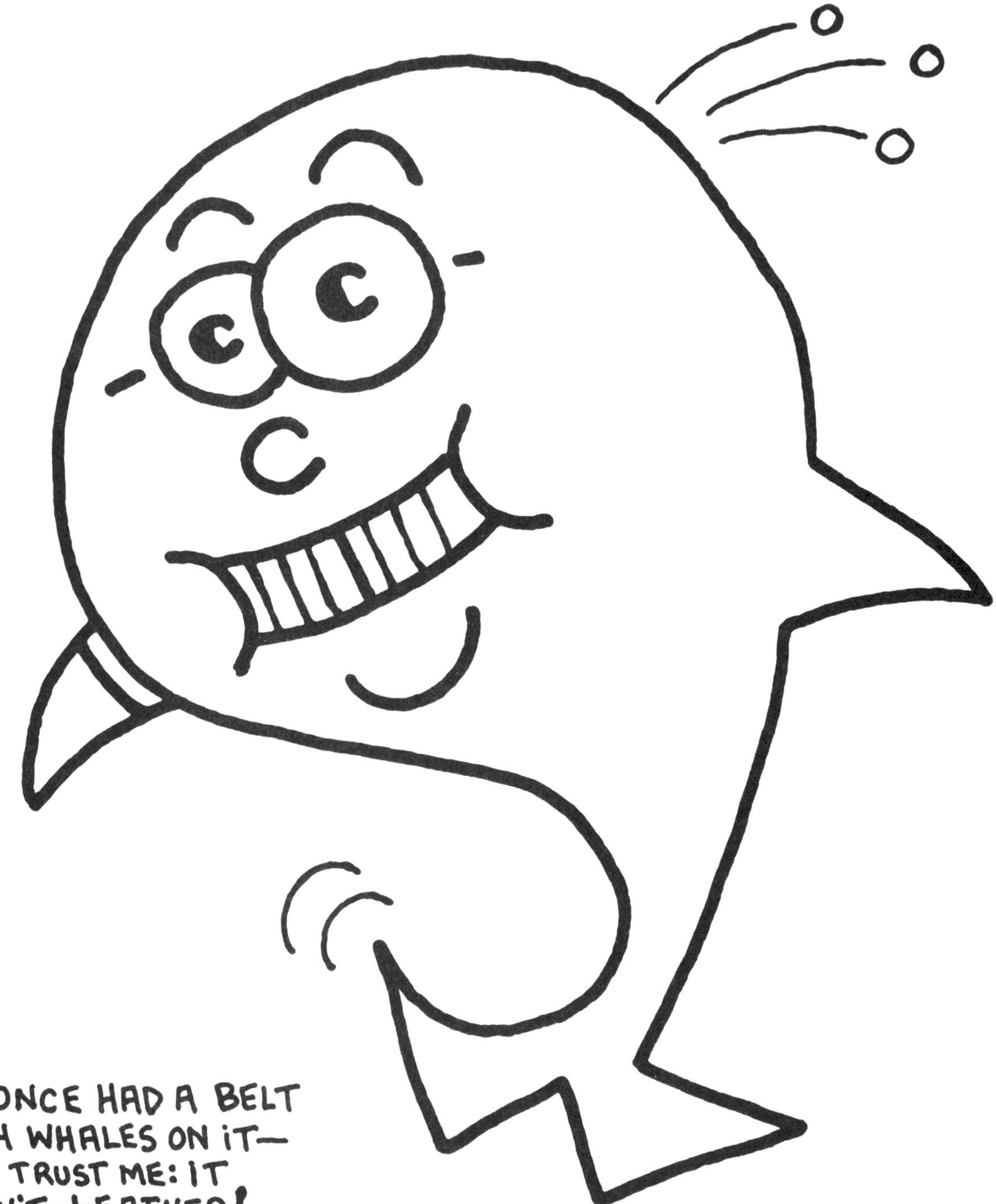

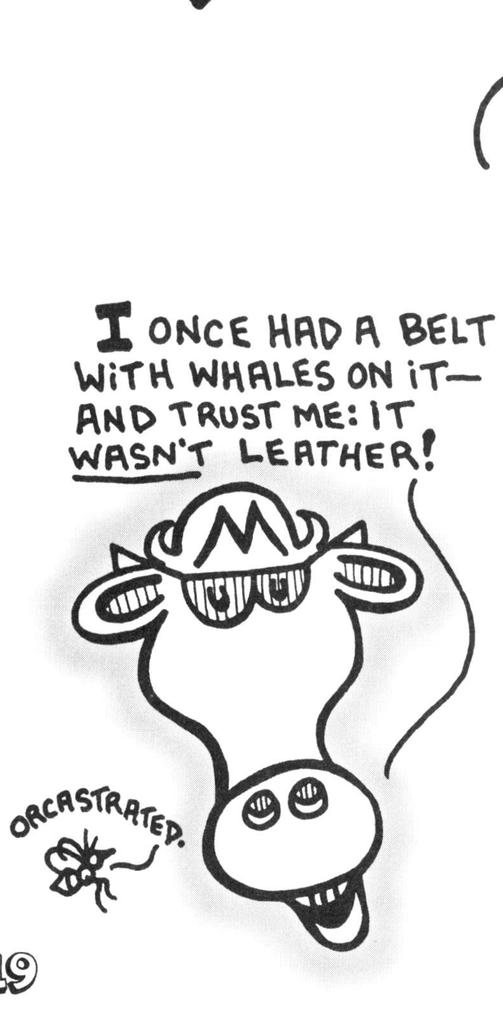

Using its beautiful underwater **VOiCE**, this **WHALE** sings a tune and keeps time by tapping its tail. Its songs provide a lively soundtrack for the ocean's food chain.

WHALE'S VOiCE

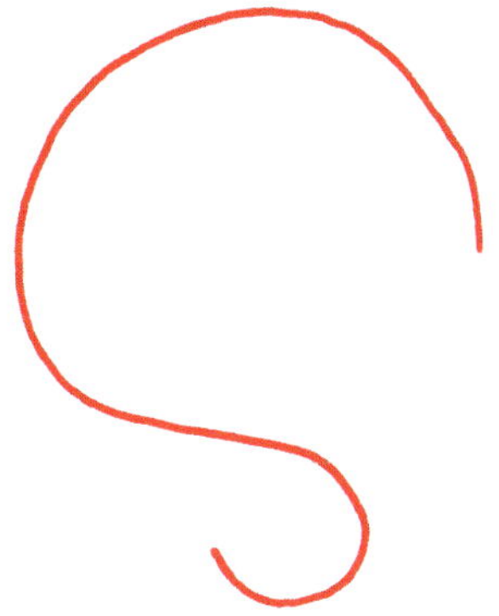

1

WHALE'S VOiCE

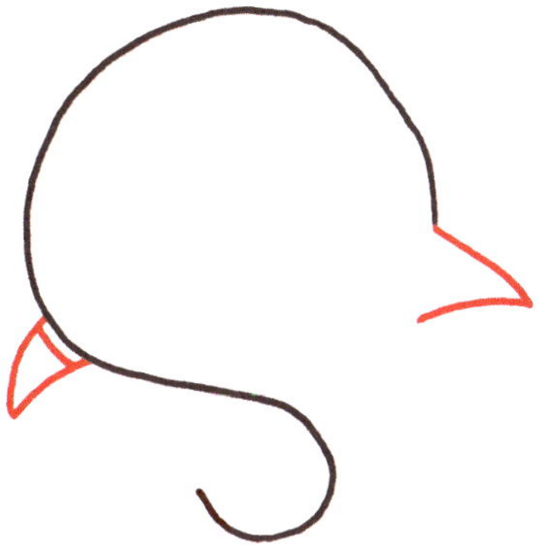

2

WHALE'S VOiCE

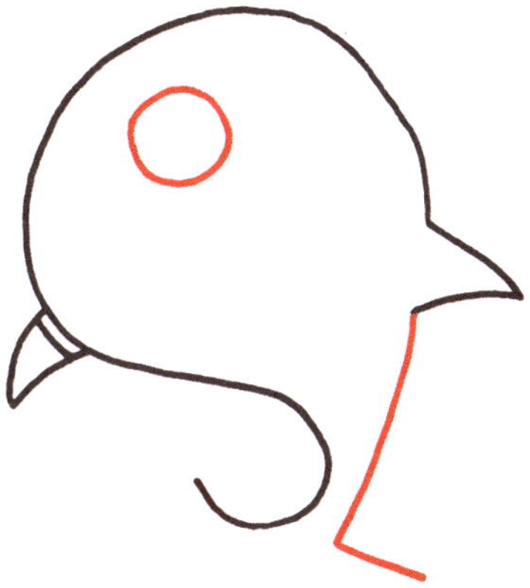

3

WHALE'S VOiCE

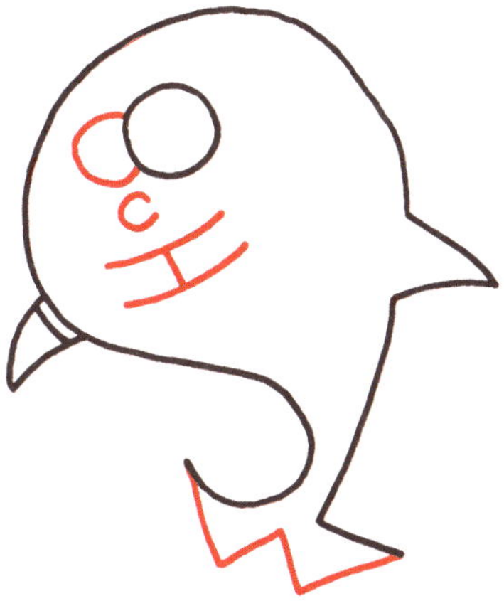

4

WHALE'S VOiCE

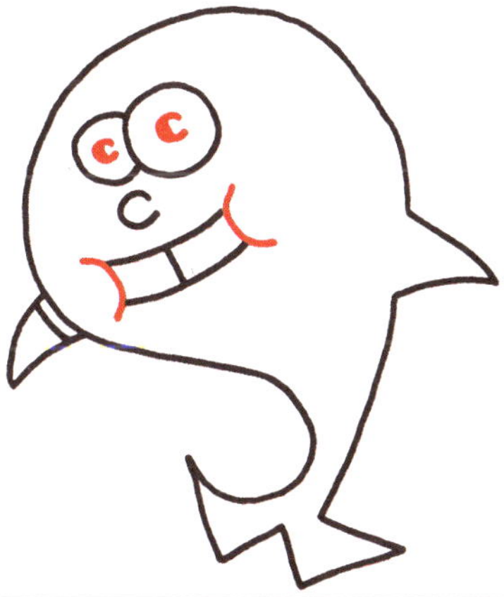

5

WHALE'S VOiCE

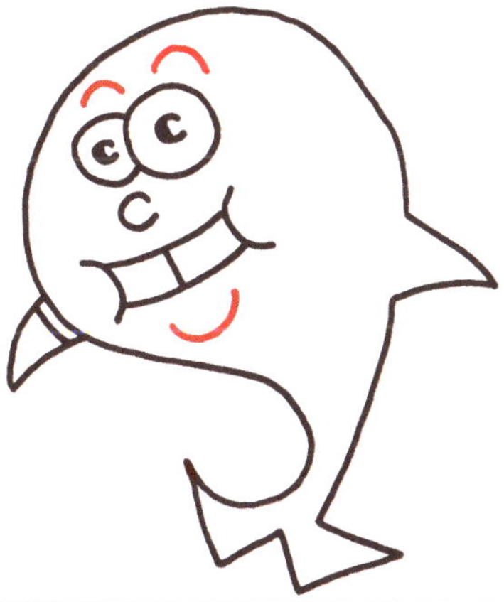

6

WHALE'S VOiCE

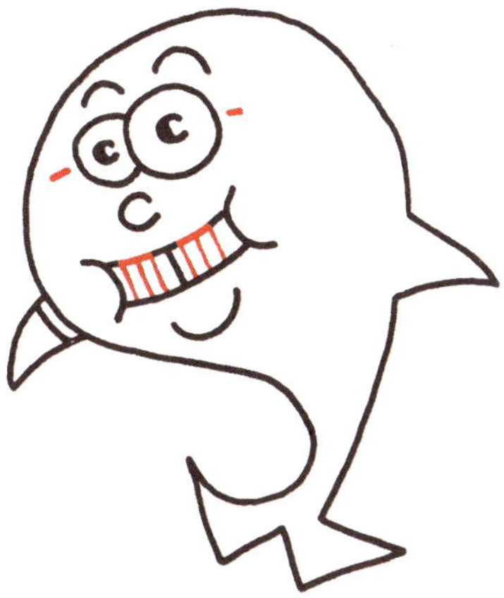

7

WHALE'S VOiCE

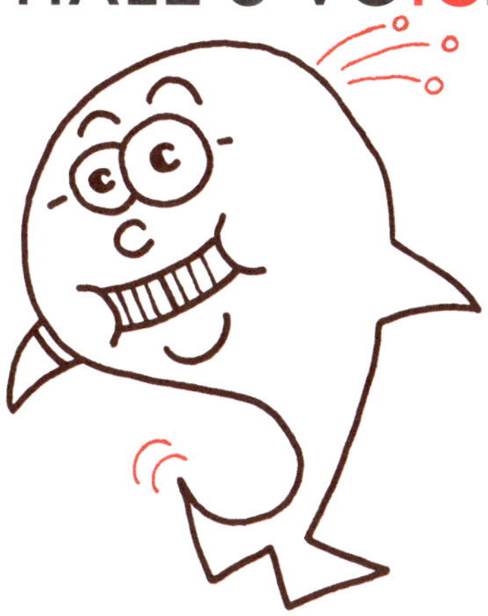

8

THE **BE COOL** KiD

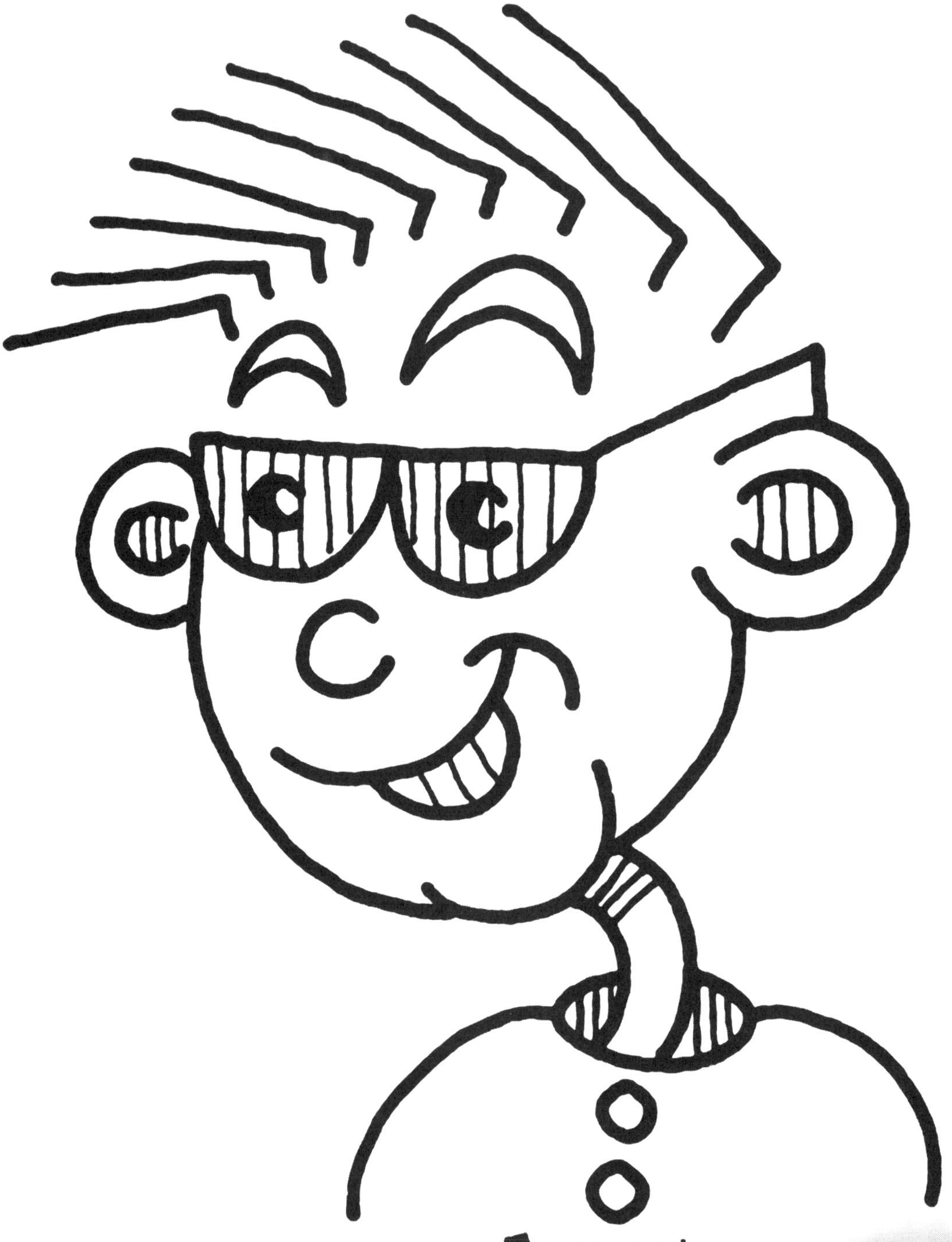

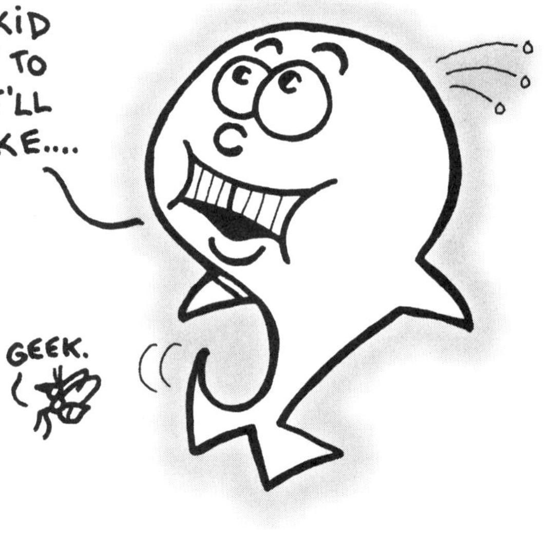

With his sunglasses, raised eyebrow, and crooked smile, this kid's constant goal in life is to **BE COOL**. Still, casual observers aren't sure if he's just a nerd with lots of hair gel.

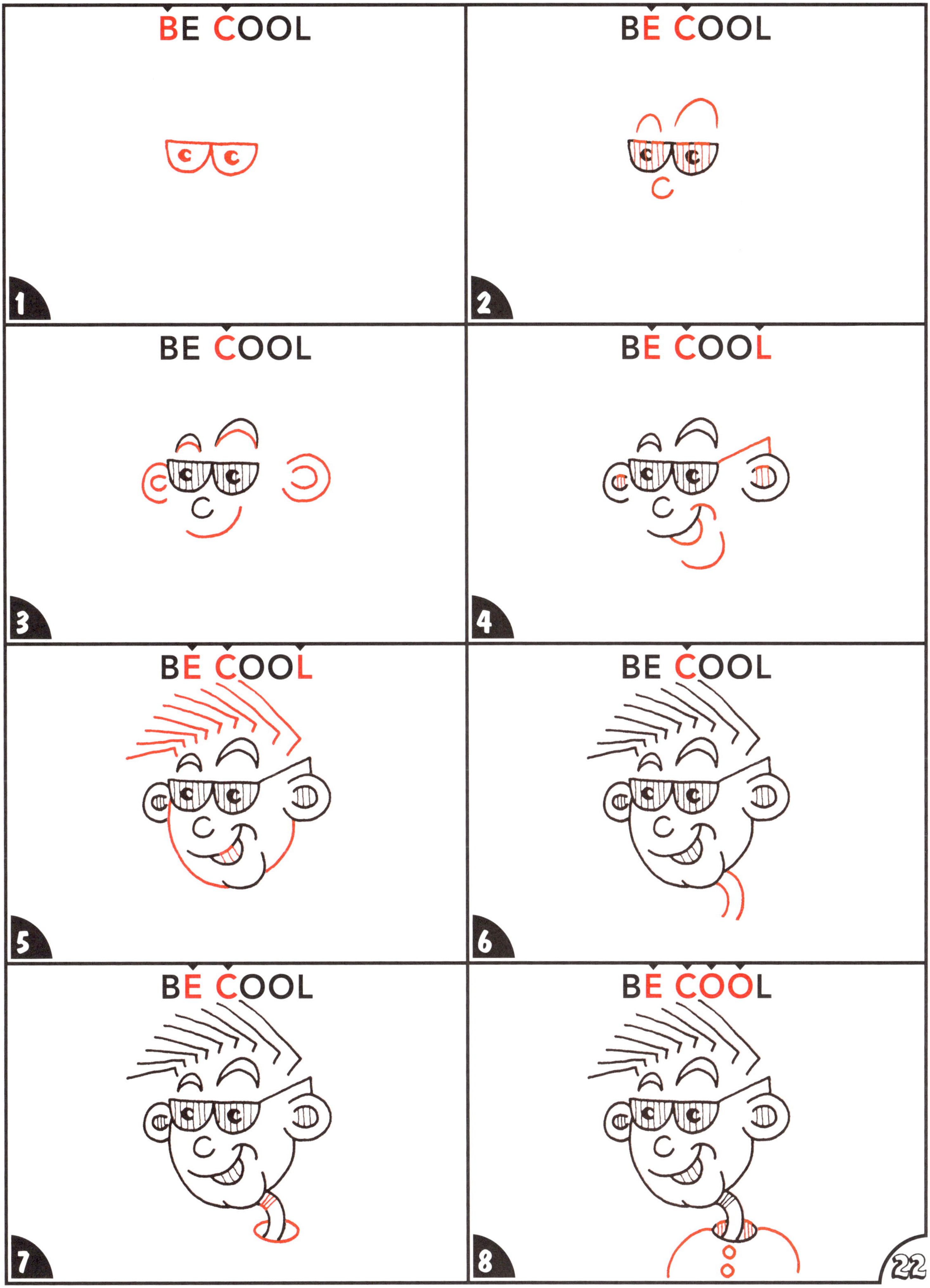
BE COOL
1
BE COOL
2
BE COOL
3
BE COOL
4
BE COOL
5
BE COOL
6
BE COOL
7
BE COOL
8

THE CLOUD NiNE CLOUD

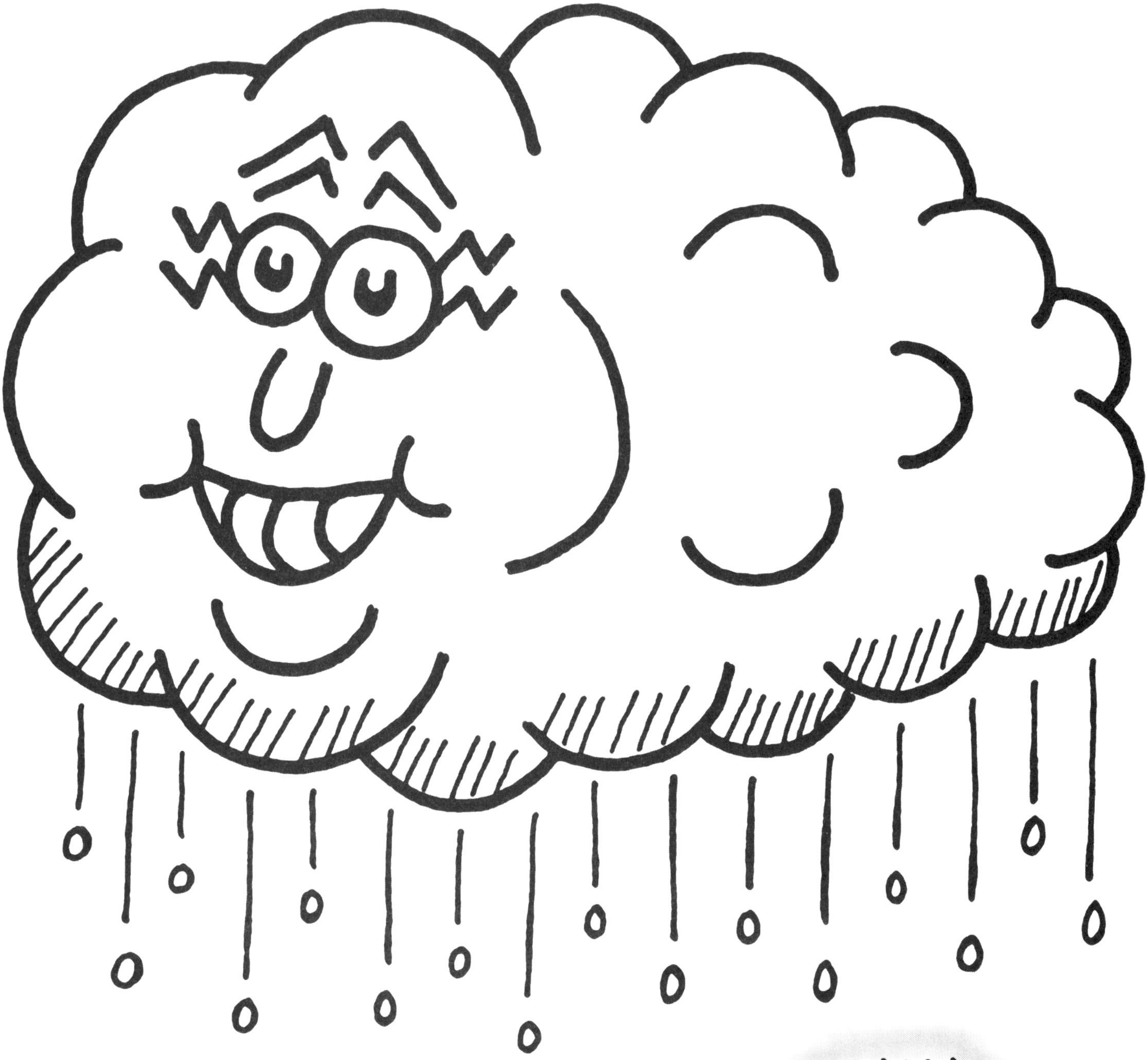

This very happy, puffy, cloud is a favorite with farmers who enjoy its gentle showers. Seeing their crops grow healthy puts them on **CLOUD NiNE**.

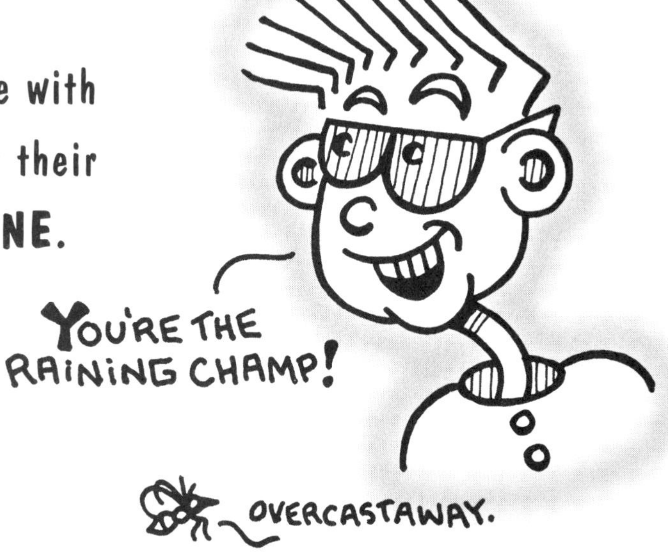

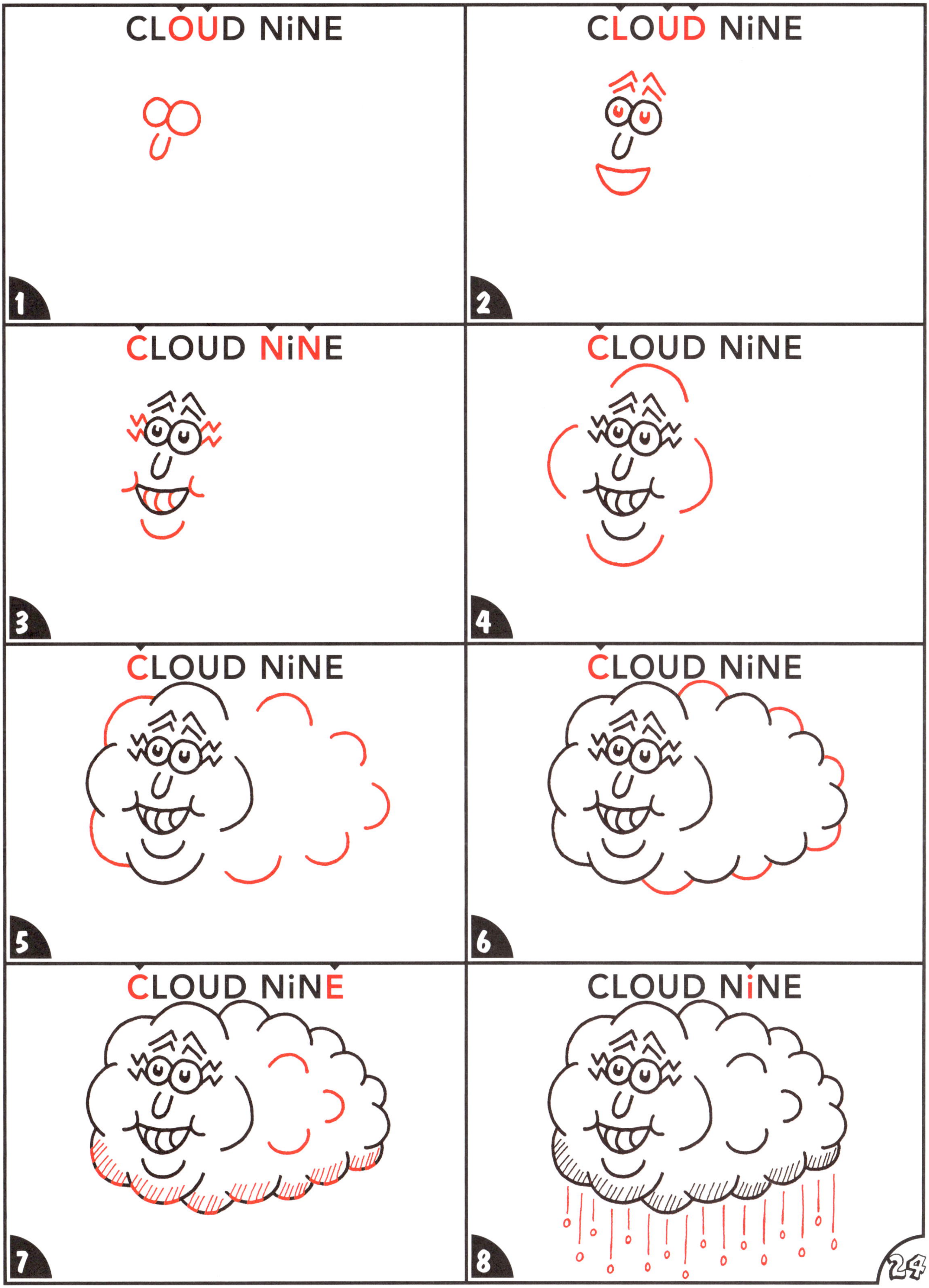
CLOUD NiNE
1
CLOUD NiNE
2
CLOUD NiNE
3
CLOUD NiNE
4
CLOUD NiNE
5
CLOUD NiNE
6
CLOUD NiNE
7
CLOUD NiNE
8

THE **EViL JAWS MAC** SHARK

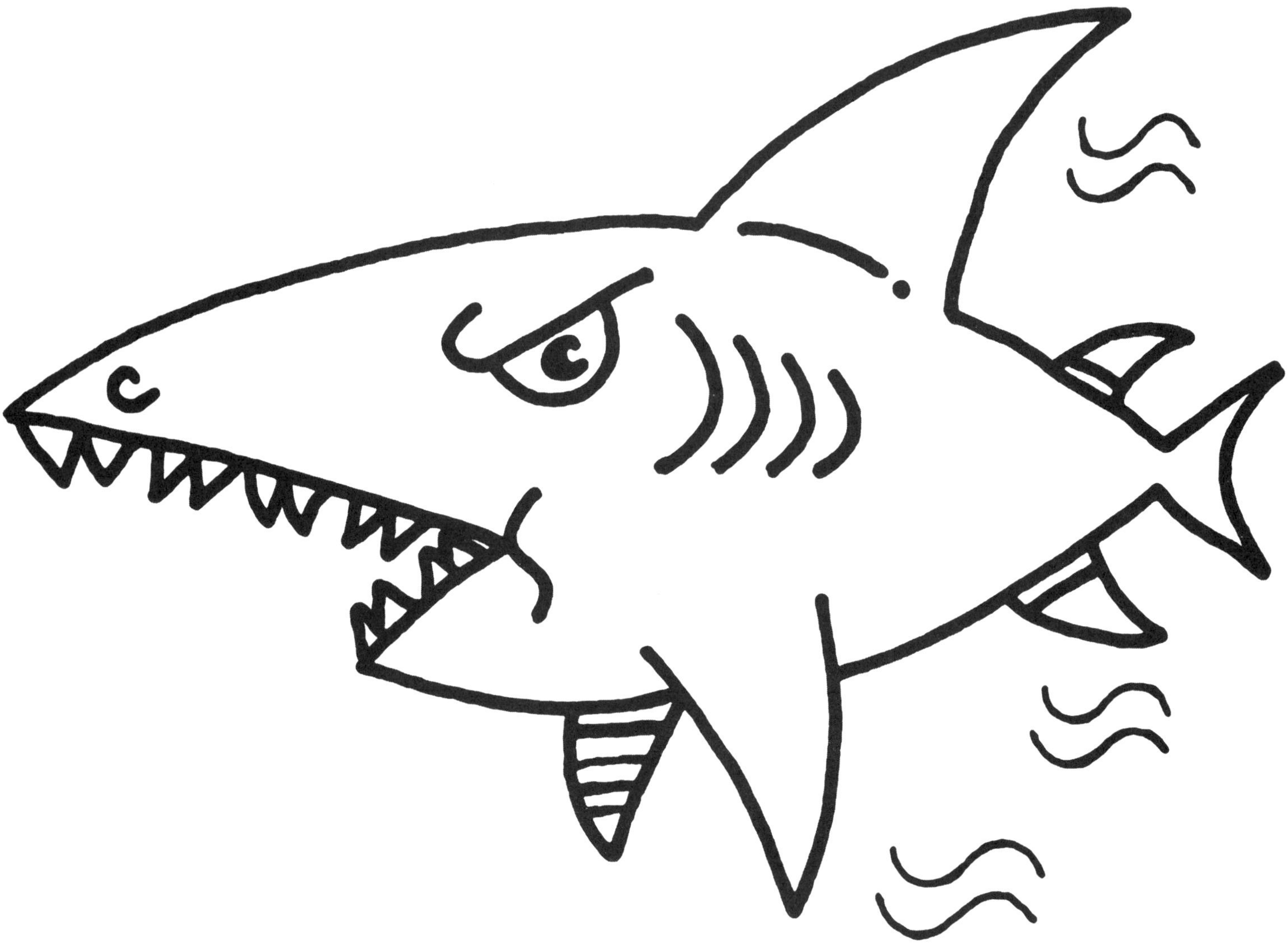

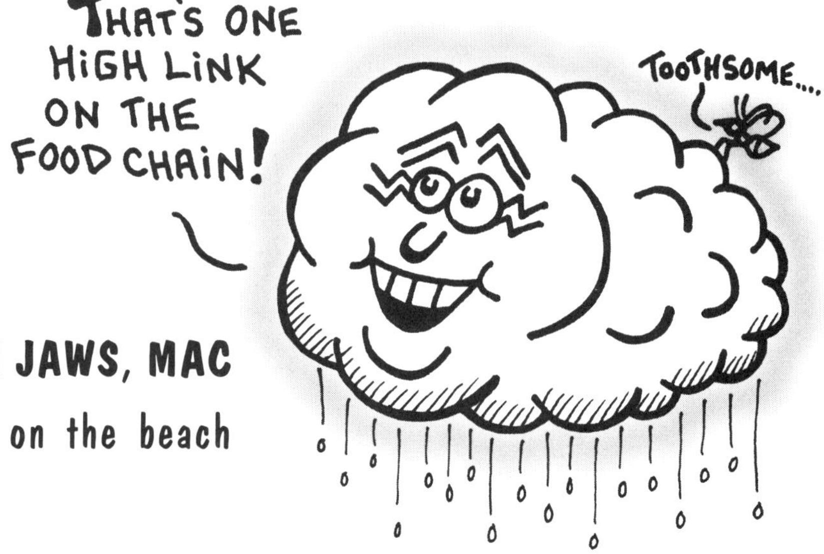

EViL looking with his tooth-filled **JAWS, MAC** is a shark who can create a frenzy on the beach with one flash of his dorsal fin.

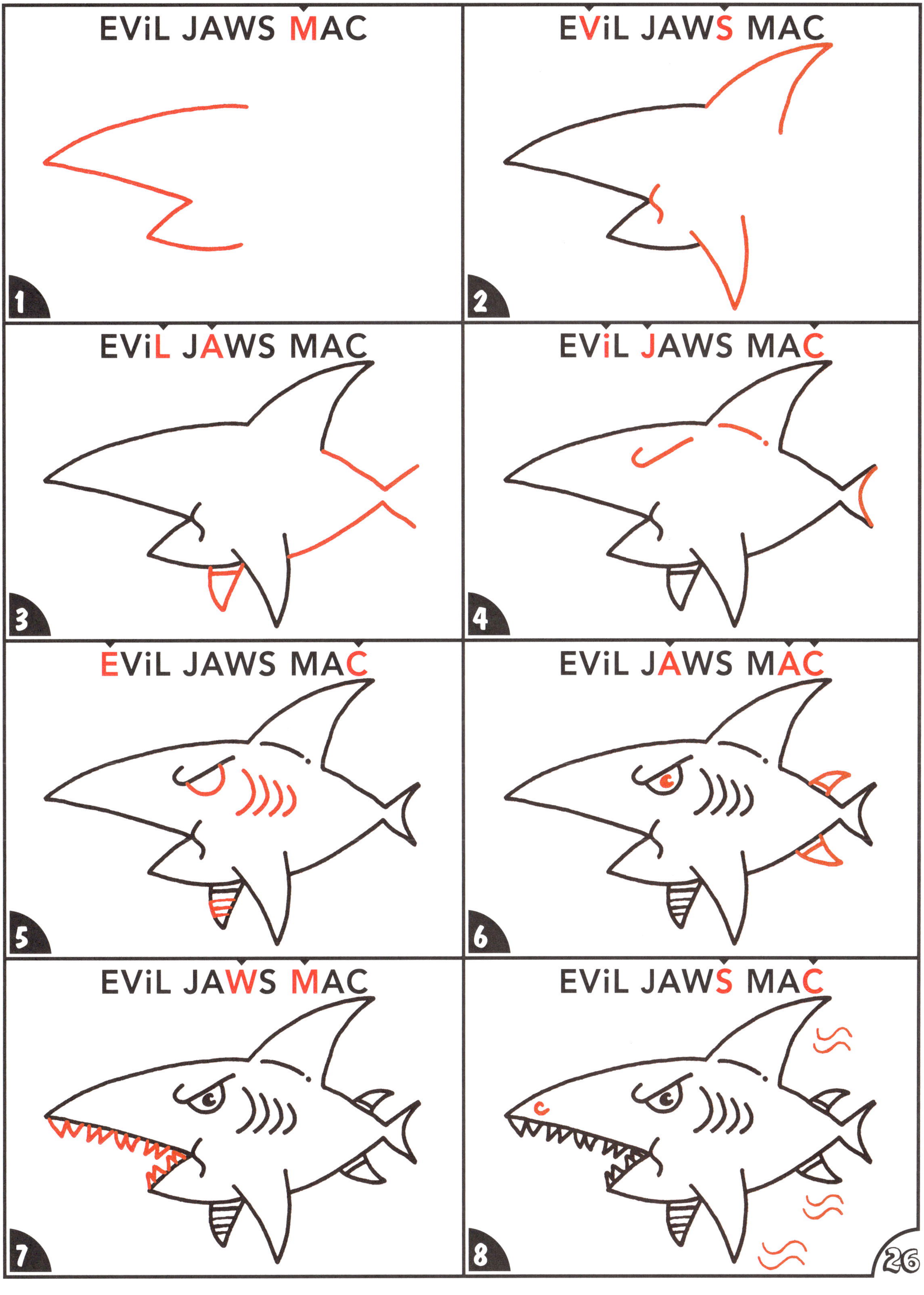
EViL JAWS MAC
1
EViL JAWS MAC
2
EViL JAWS MAC
3
EViL JAWS MAC
4
EViL JAWS MAC
5
EViL JAWS MAC
6
EViL JAWS MAC
7
EViL JAWS MAC
8

THE iCY JELLY JOE JELLYFiSH

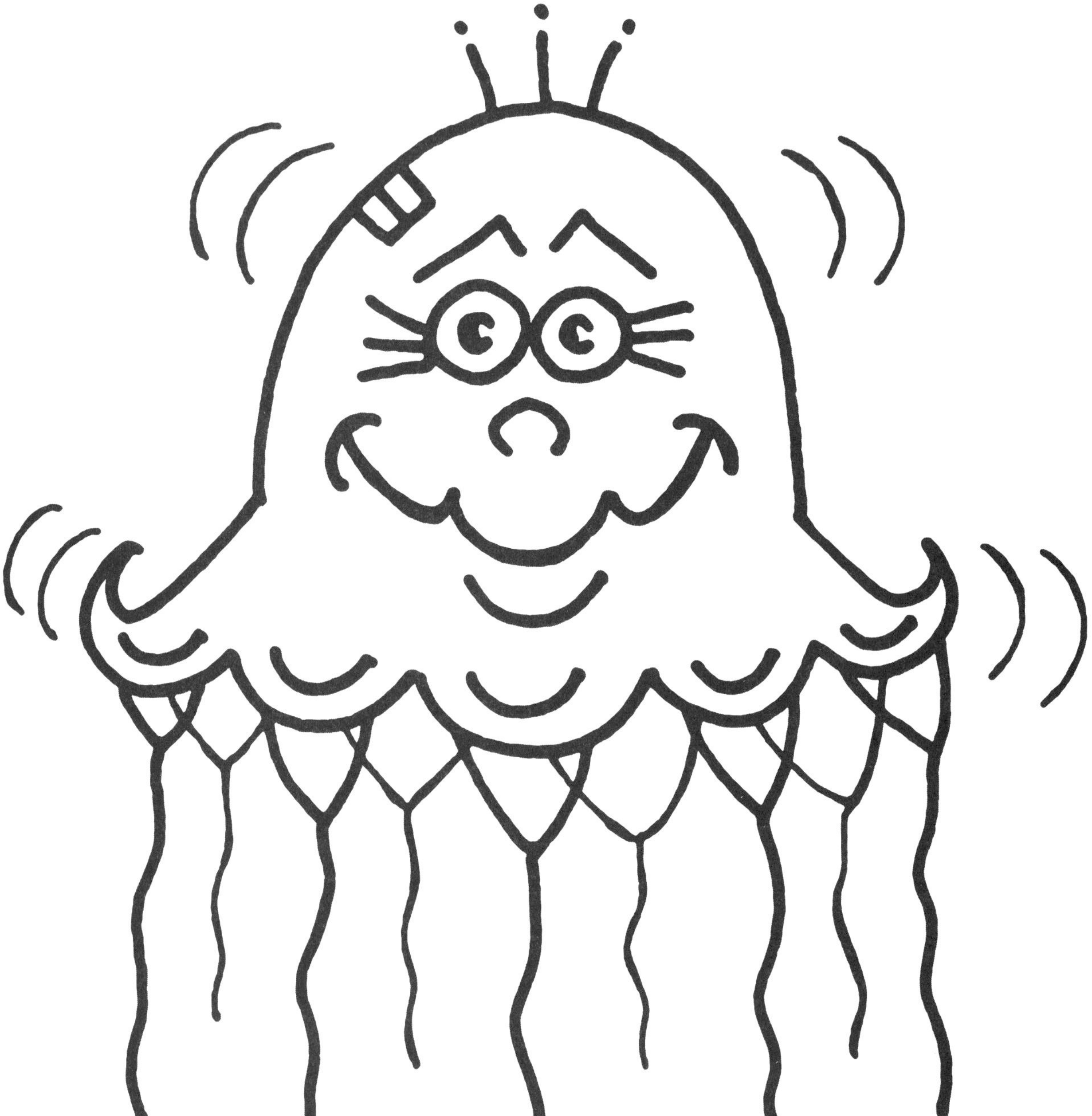

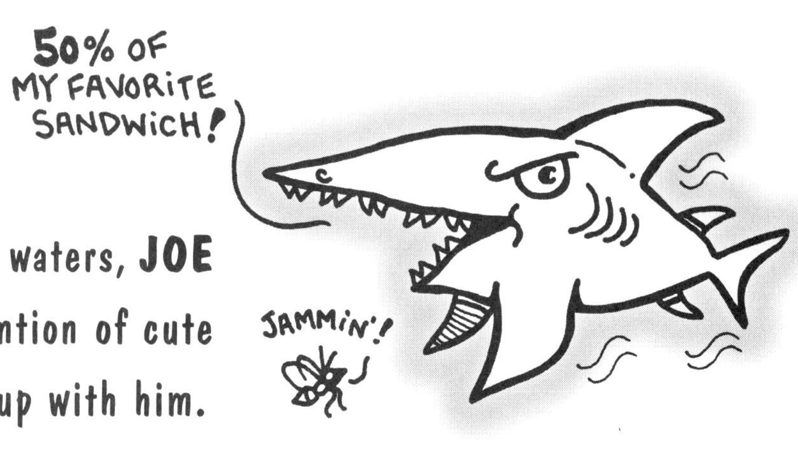

Moving gracefully through the **iCY** waters, **JOE** the **JELLY**fish often catches the attention of cute peanutbutterfish, who long to mix it up with him.

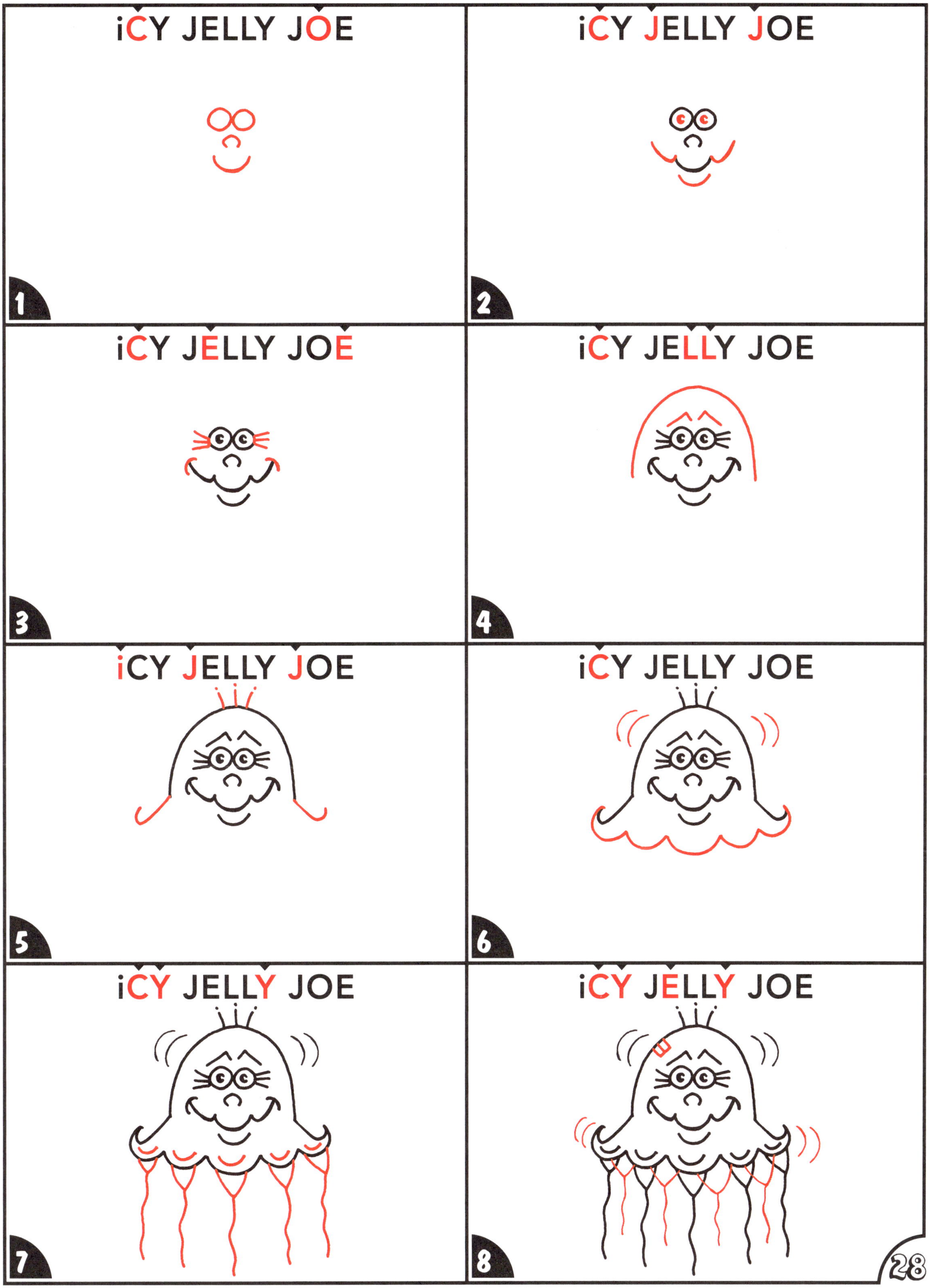
iCY JELLY JOE
1
iCY JELLY JOE
2
iCY JELLY JOE
3
iCY JELLY JOE
4
iCY JELLY JOE
5
iCY JELLY JOE
6
iCY JELLY JOE
7
iCY JELLY JOE
8

THE SLOW PACE TURTLE

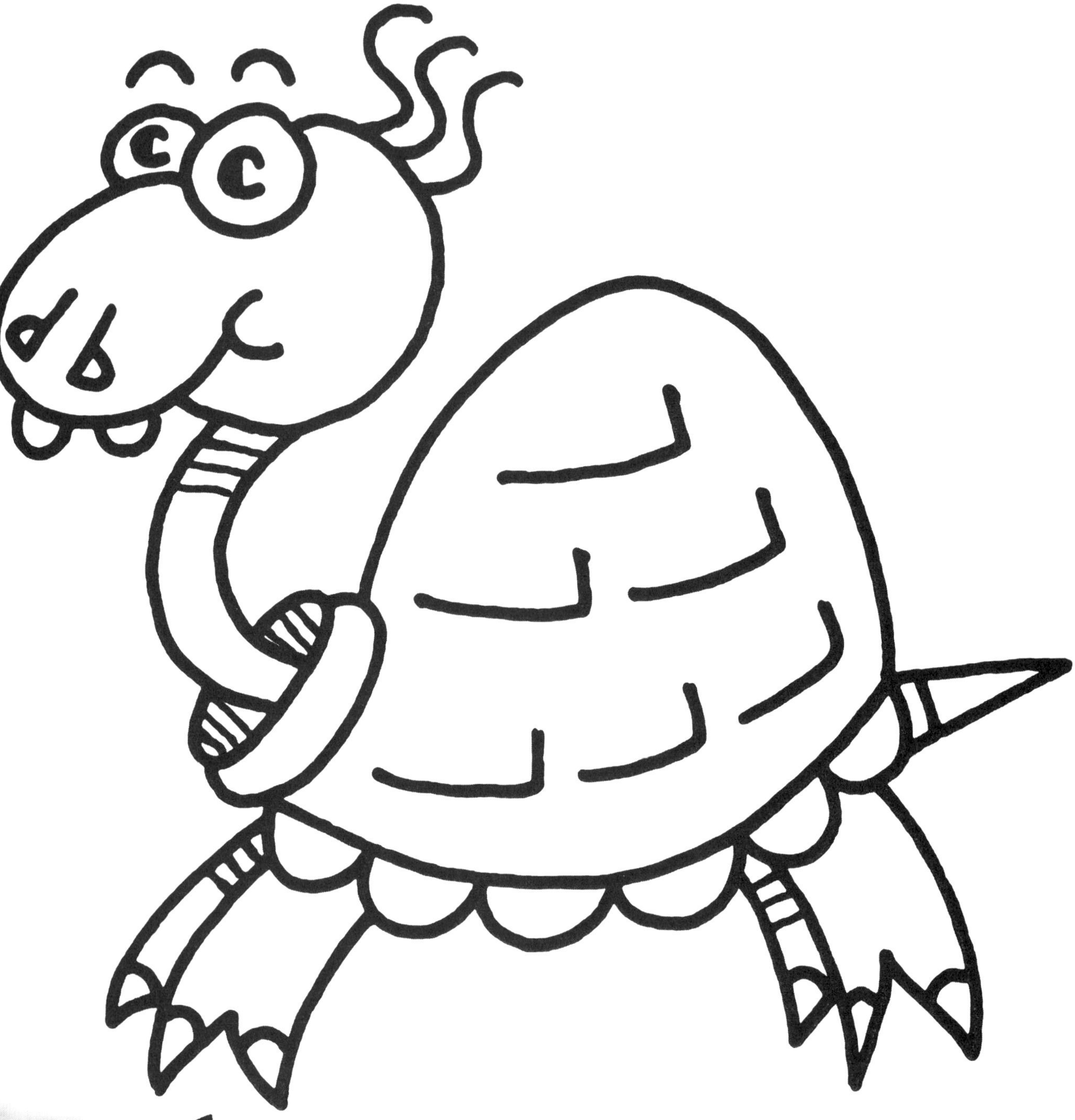

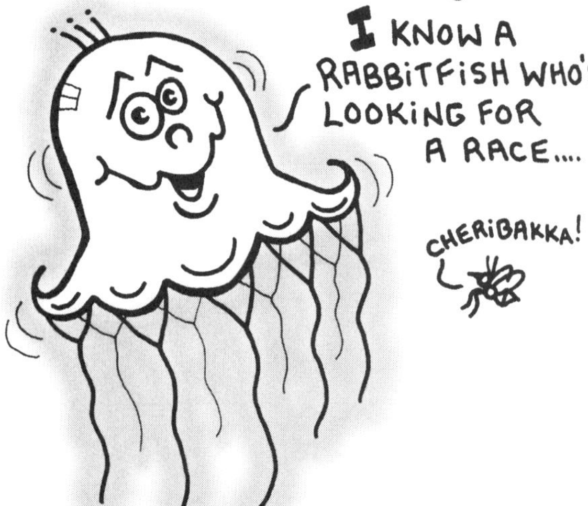

When you carry your house around with you, like this turtle, you can't expect to move at more than a **SLOW PACE**. The advantage is, wherever you are, you are home.

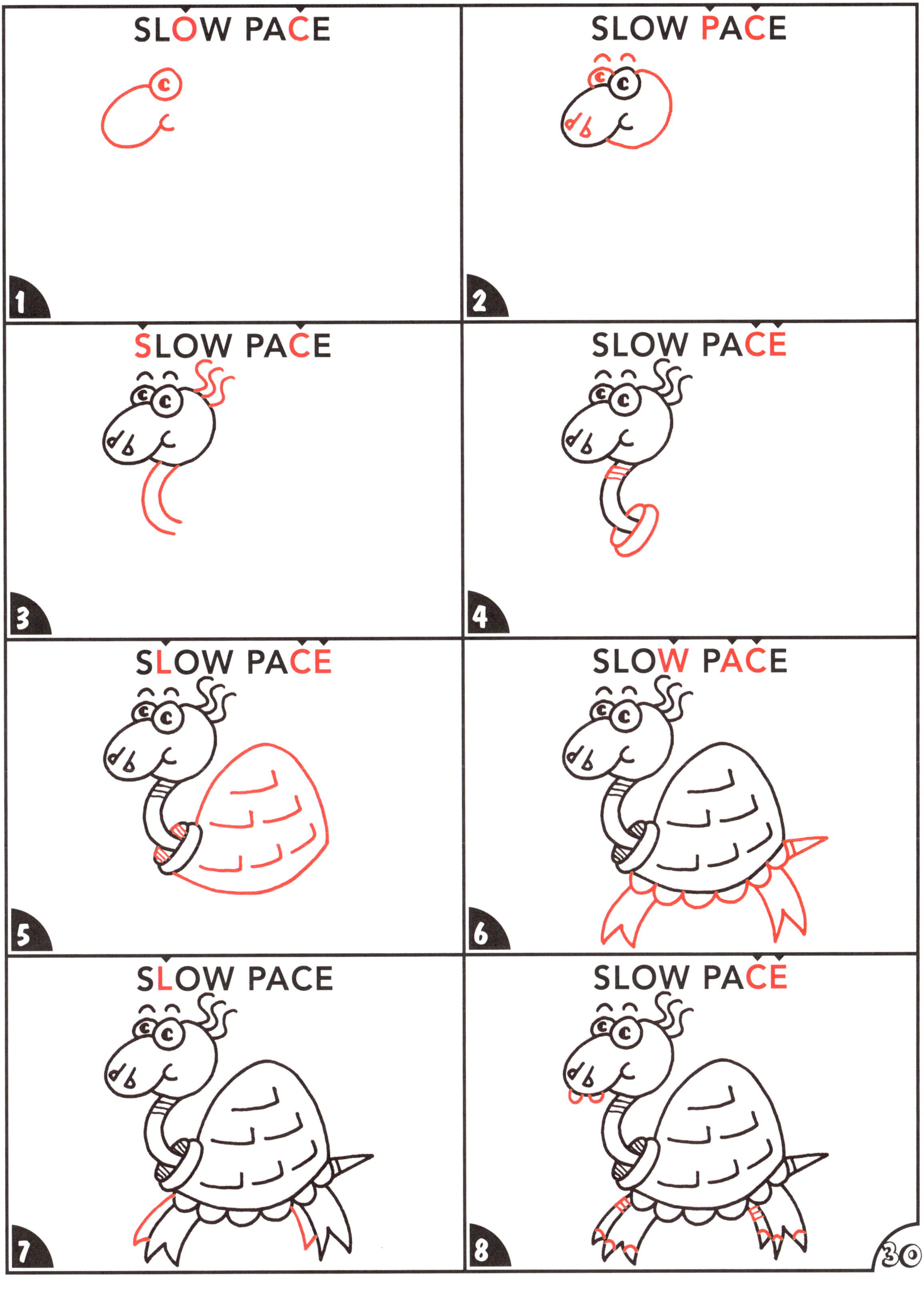
SLOW PACE
1
SLOW PACE
2
SLOW PACE
3
SLOW PACE
4
SLOW PACE
5
SLOW PACE
6
SLOW PACE
7
SLOW PACE
8

THE ViC'S WEB SPiDER

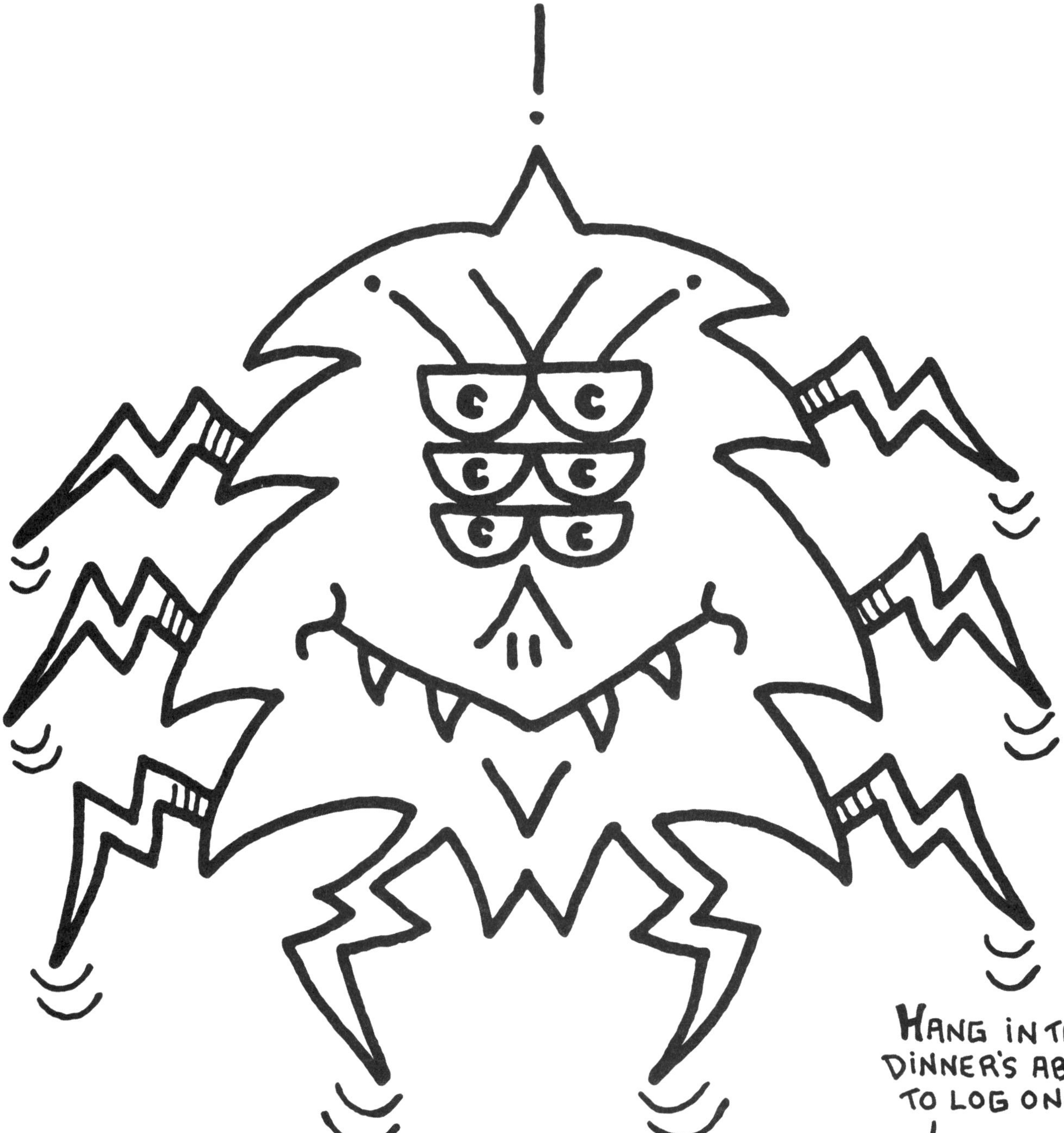

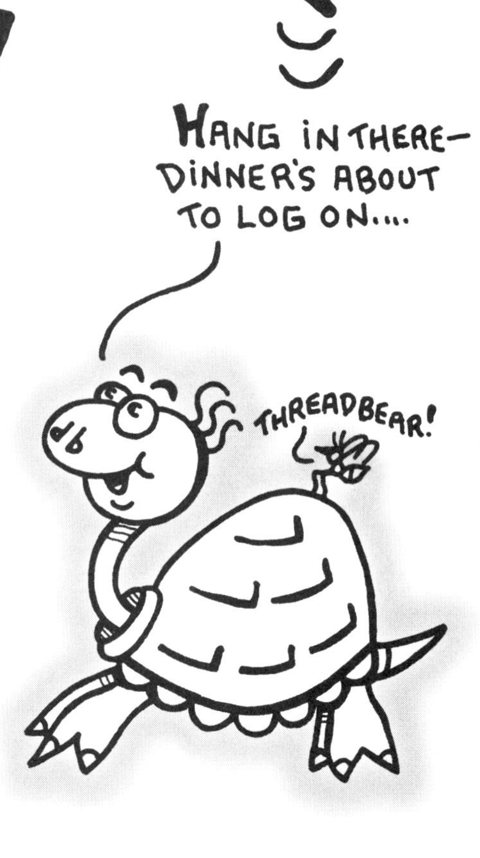

It is an unfortunate fly that bumbles into **ViC'S** spider **WEB**. Few of his guests get to tell about their visits.

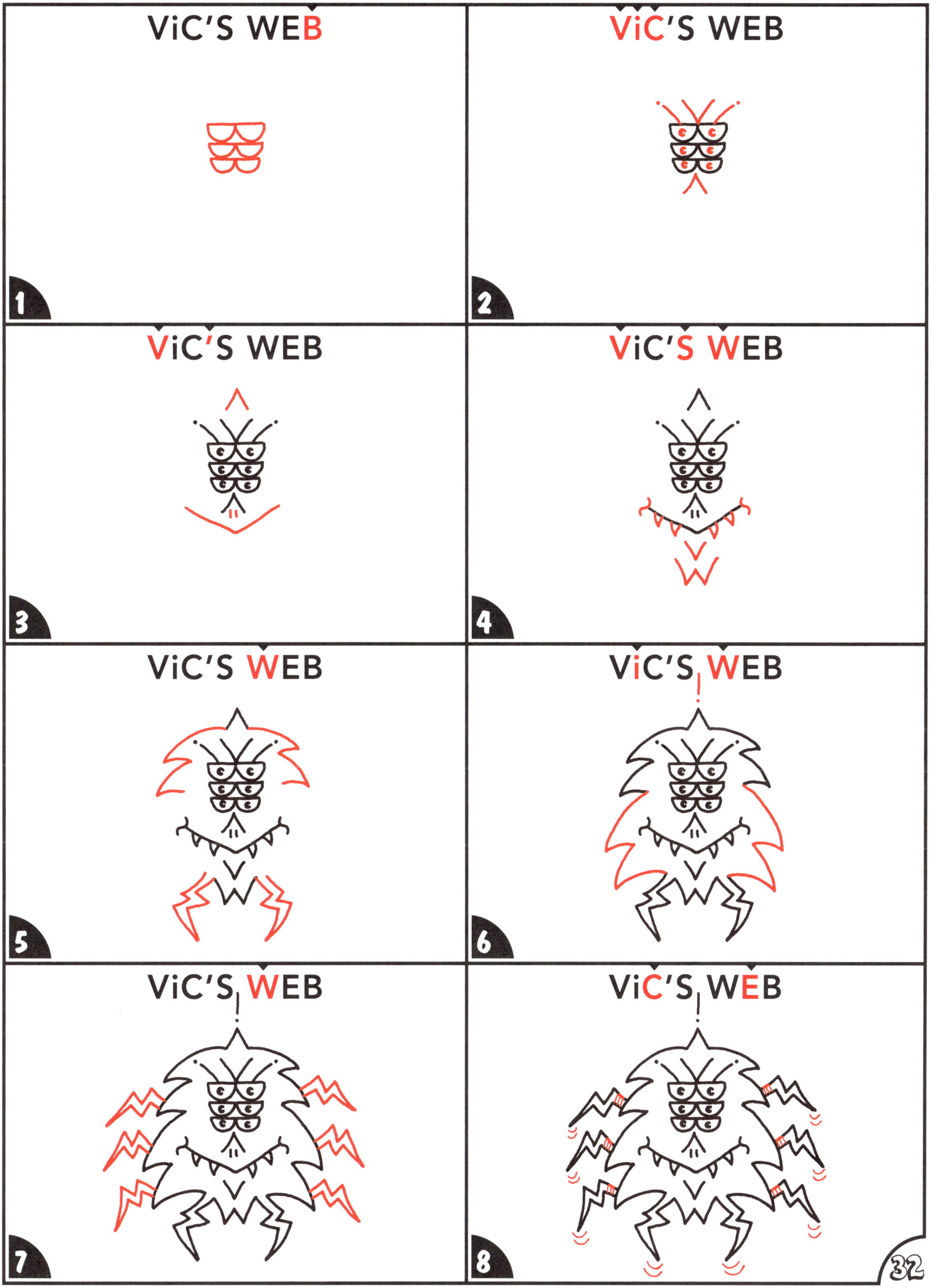
ViC'S WEB
1
ViC'S WEB
2
ViC'S WEB
3
ViC'S WEB
4
ViC'S WEB
5
ViC'S WEB
6
ViC'S WEB
7
ViC'S WEB
8

THE ViNCE COME HOME! SPACE DOG

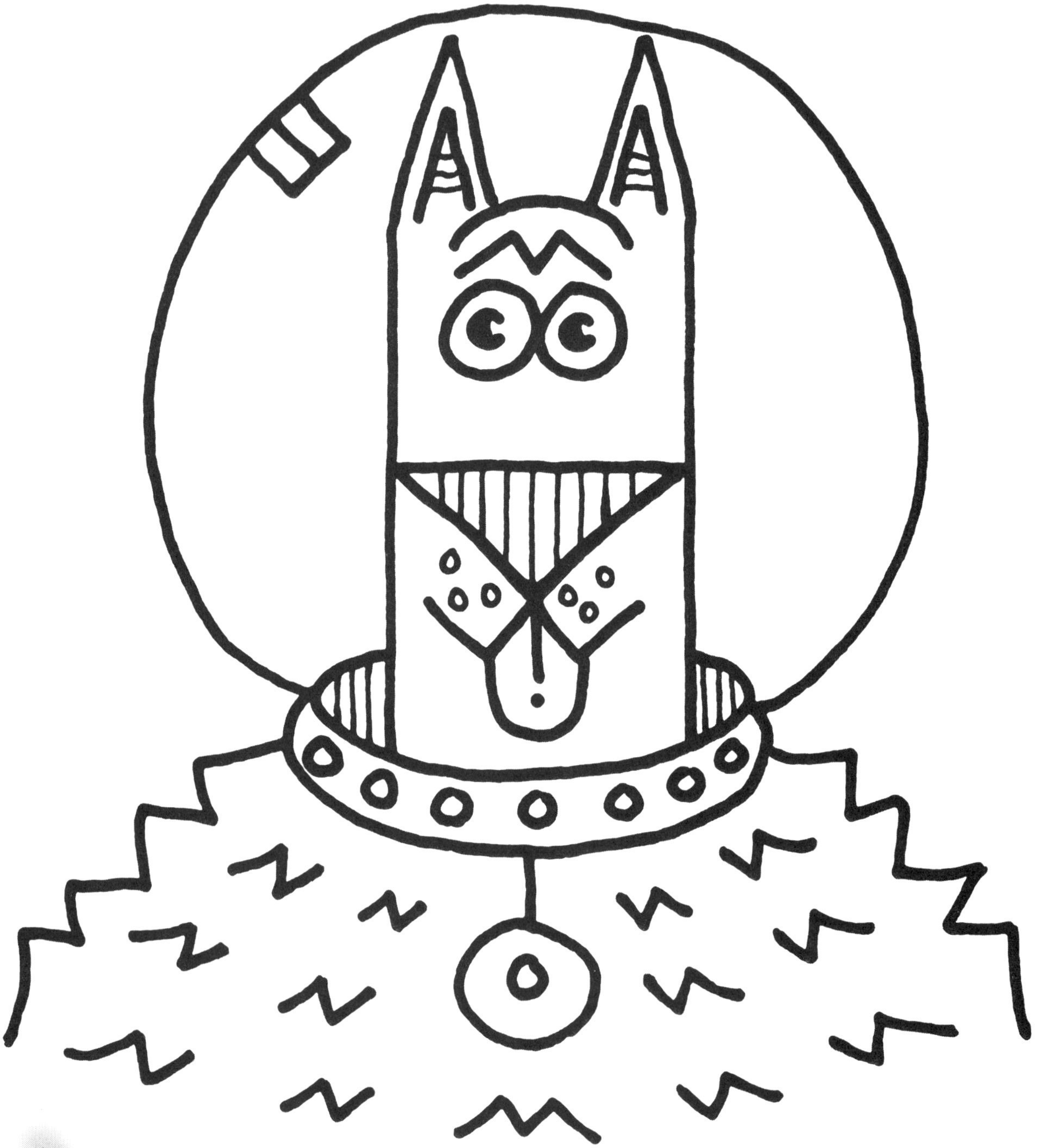

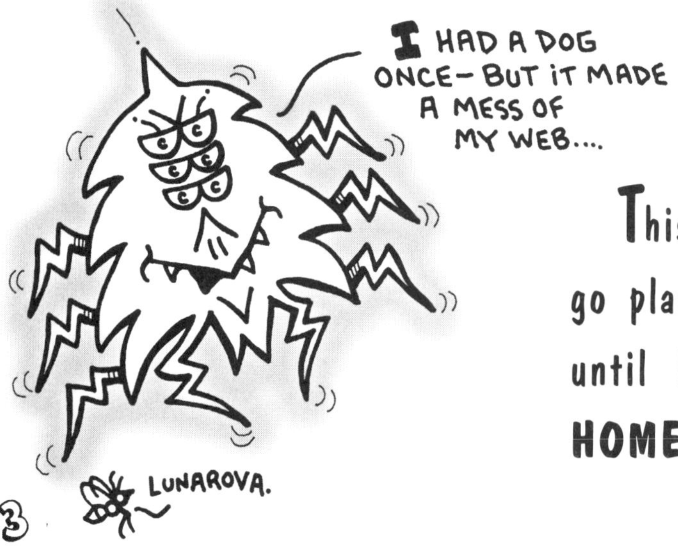

This space adventurer canine is determined to go places that no dog has gone before—that is until Mission Control signals: "**ViNCE COME HOME!**"

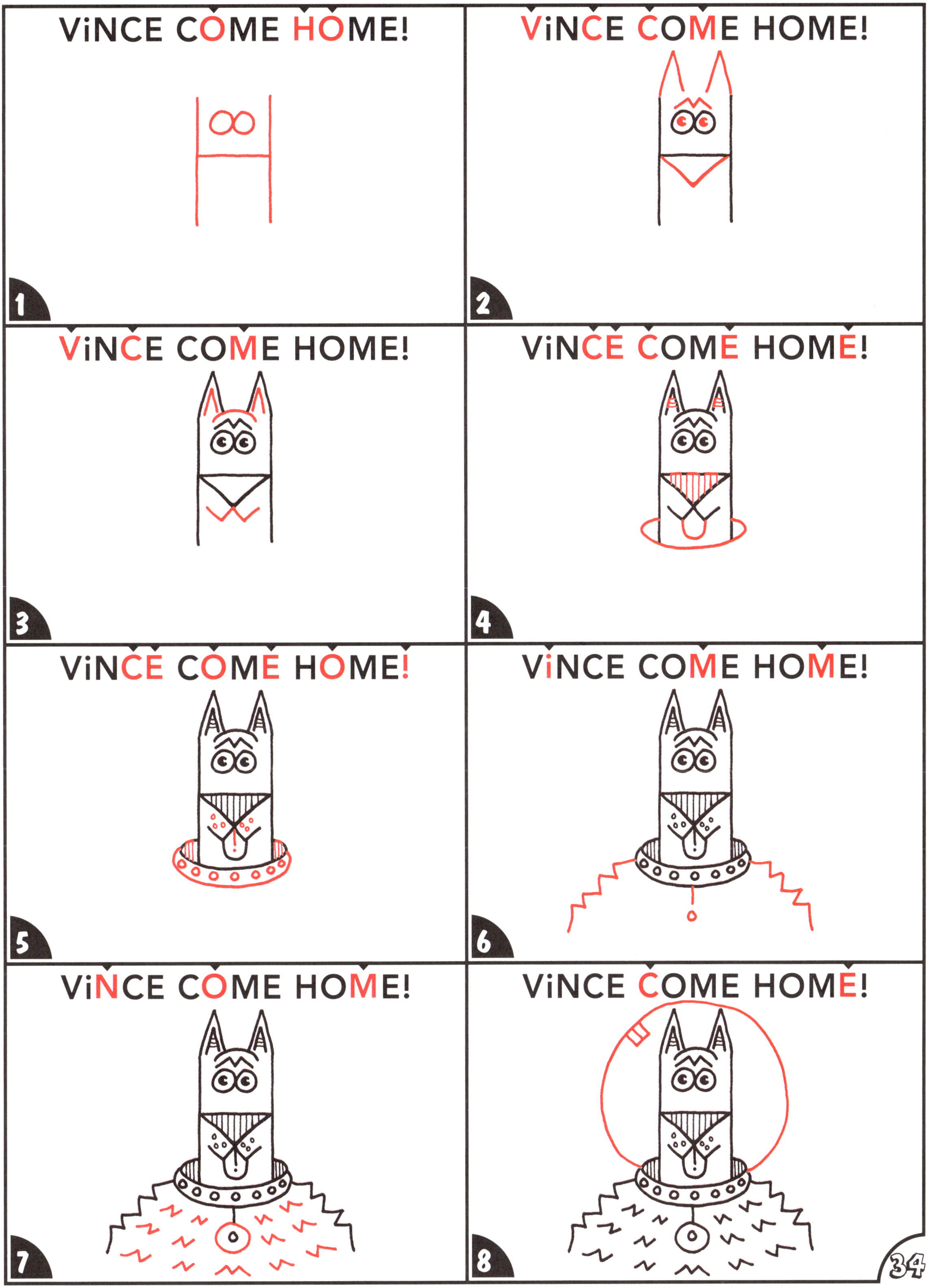
ViNCE COME HOME!
1
ViNCE COME HOME!
2
ViNCE COME HOME!
3
ViNCE COME HOME!
4
ViNCE COME HOME!
5
ViNCE COME HOME!
6
ViNCE COME HOME!
7
ViNCE COME HOME!
8

THE GUS WAS COLD LOBSTER

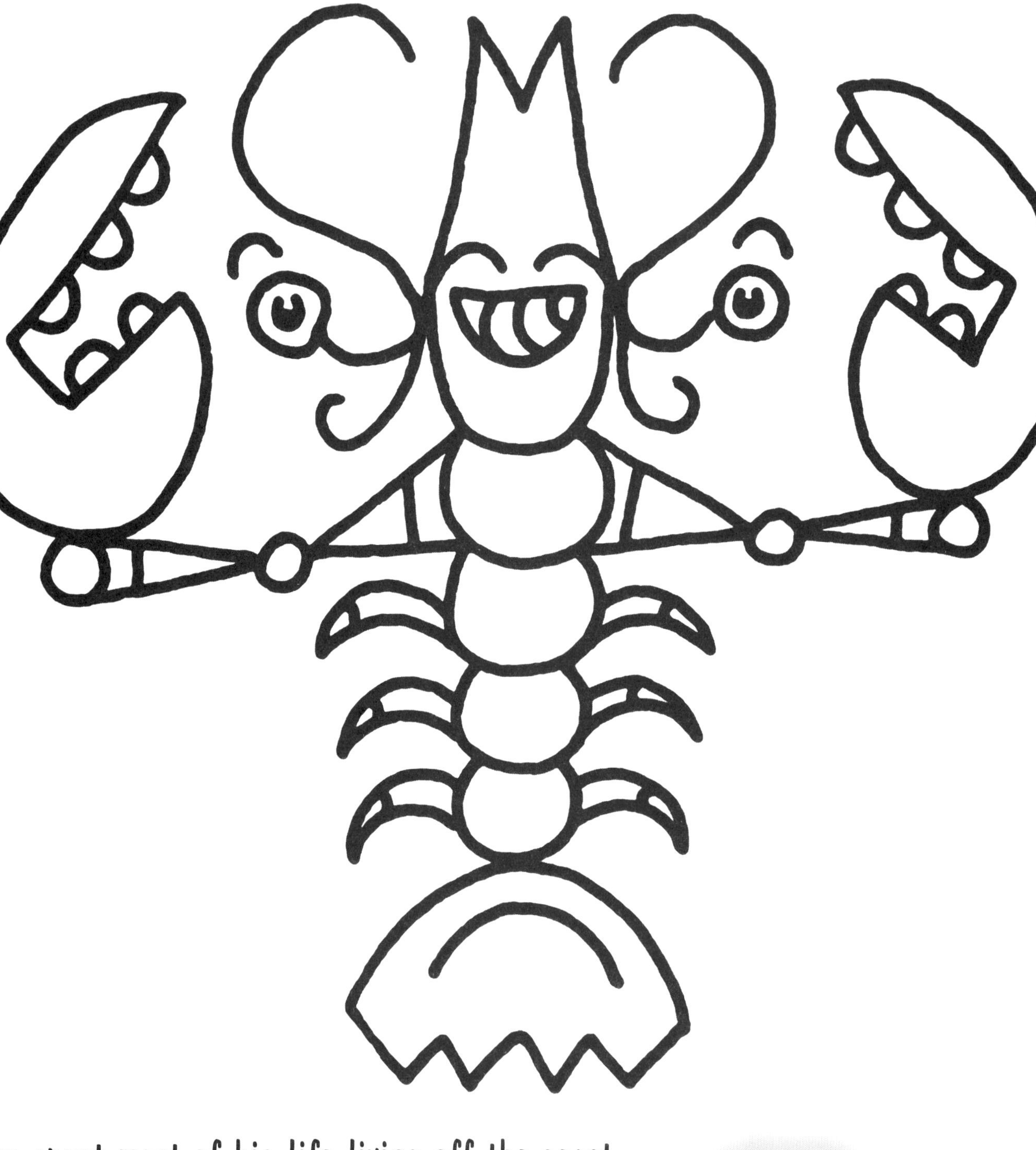

Gus spent most of his life living off the coast of Maine where the water temperature created a problem: **GUS WAS COLD**. However, this wily crustacean found a way to hitch a ride to the warm waters off Mexico, where he celebrated by growing a mustache.

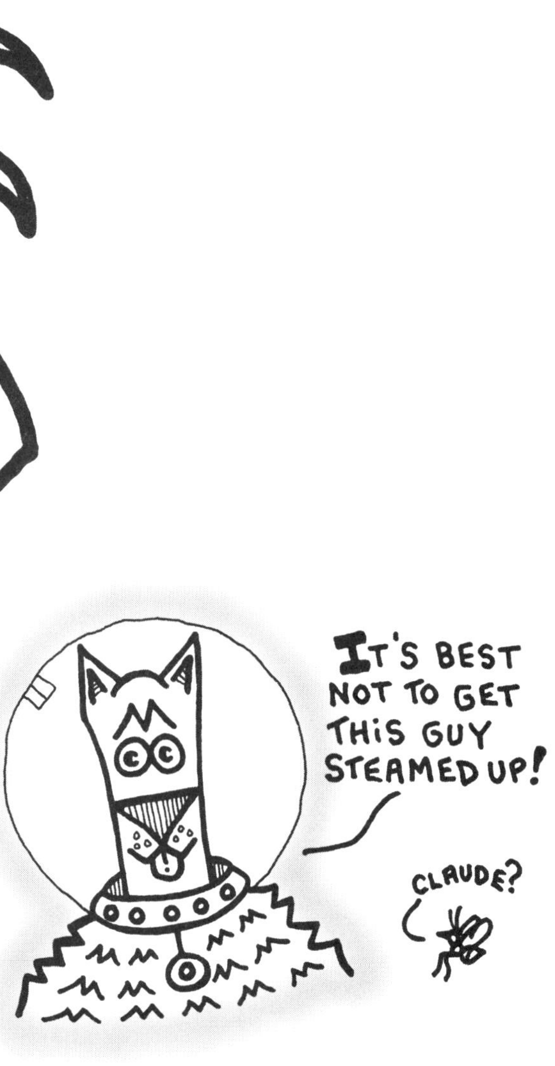

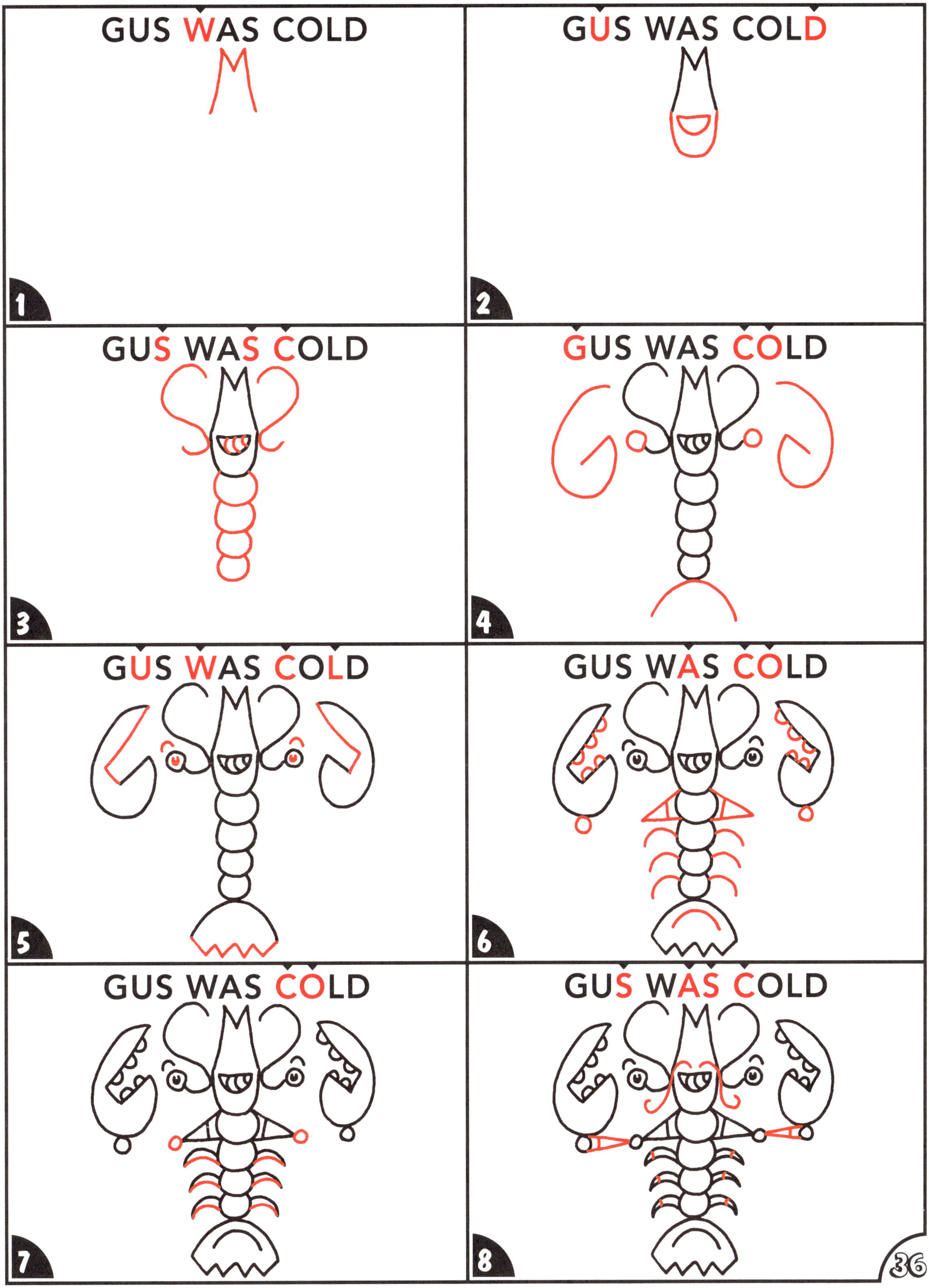
GUS WAS COLD
1
GUS WAS COLD
2
GUS WAS COLD
3
GUS WAS COLD
4
GUS WAS COLD
5
GUS WAS COLD
6
GUS WAS COLD
7
GUS WAS COLD
8

THE SOW'S VOiCE PiG

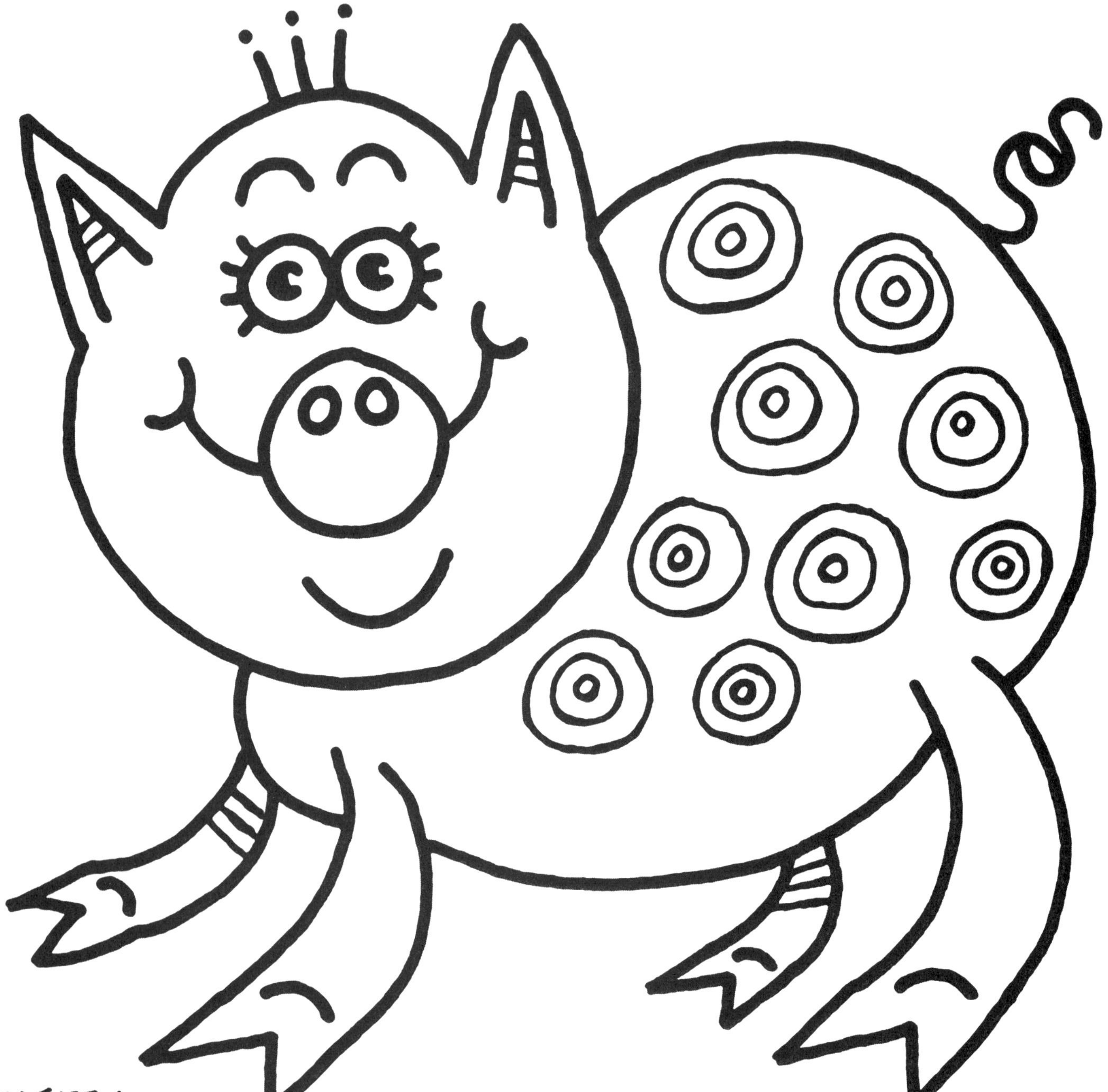

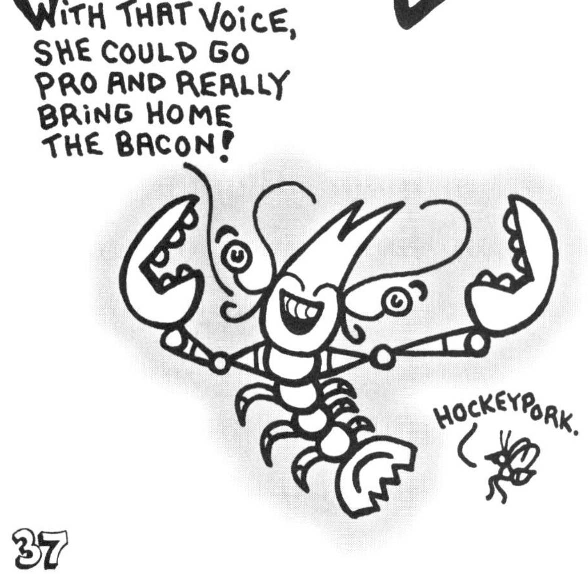

This pretty and plump female pig, or **SOW**, has a remarkably melodious singing **VOiCE**. She often gets together after-hours in the barnyard to belt out duets with the BLUES COW, with whom she plans to record.

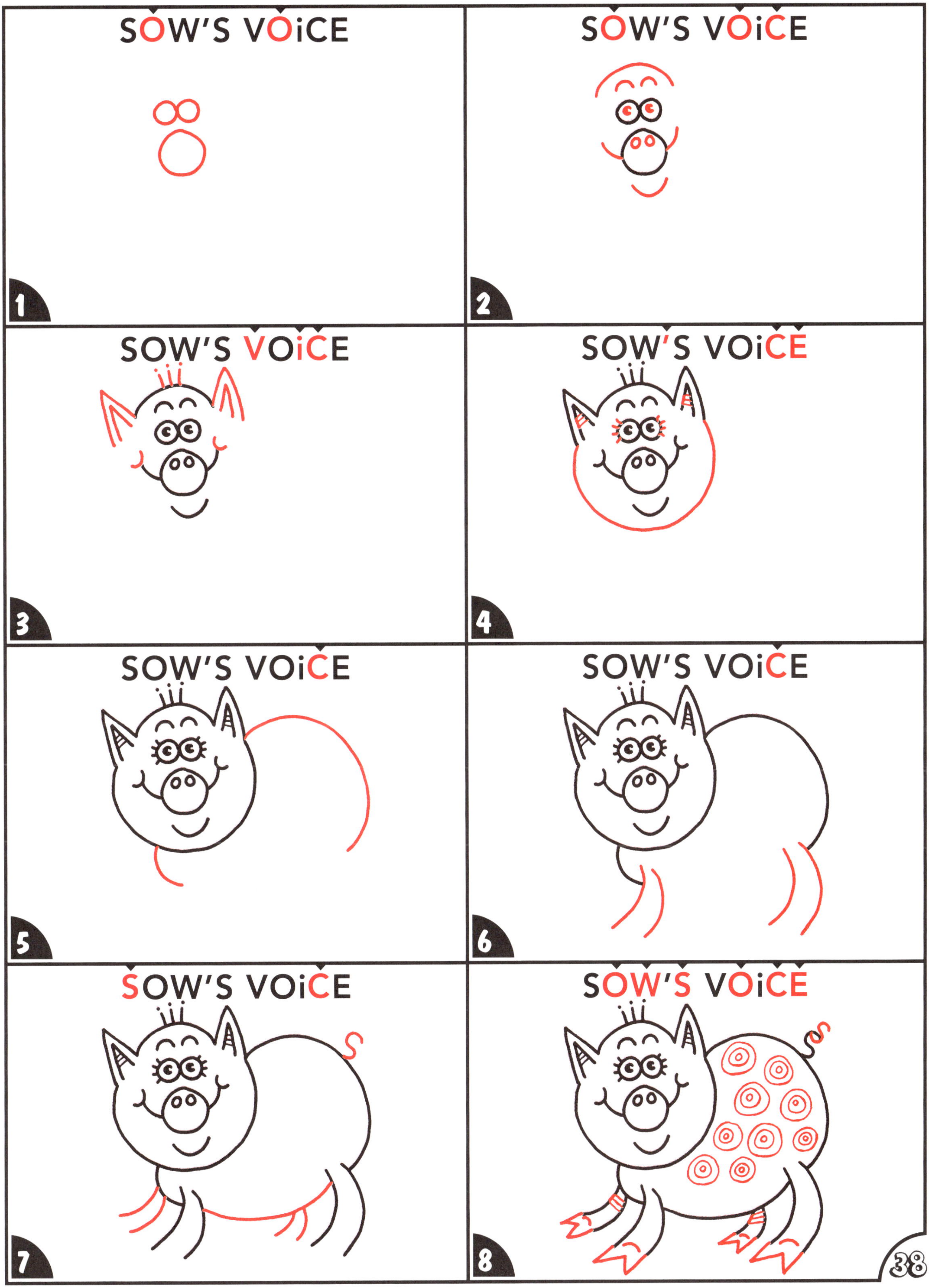
SOW'S VOiCE
1
SOW'S VOiCE
2
SOW'S VOiCE
3
SOW'S VOiCE
4
SOW'S VOiCE
5
SOW'S VOiCE
6
SOW'S VOiCE
7
SOW'S VOiCE
8

THE WAVY COURT JESTER

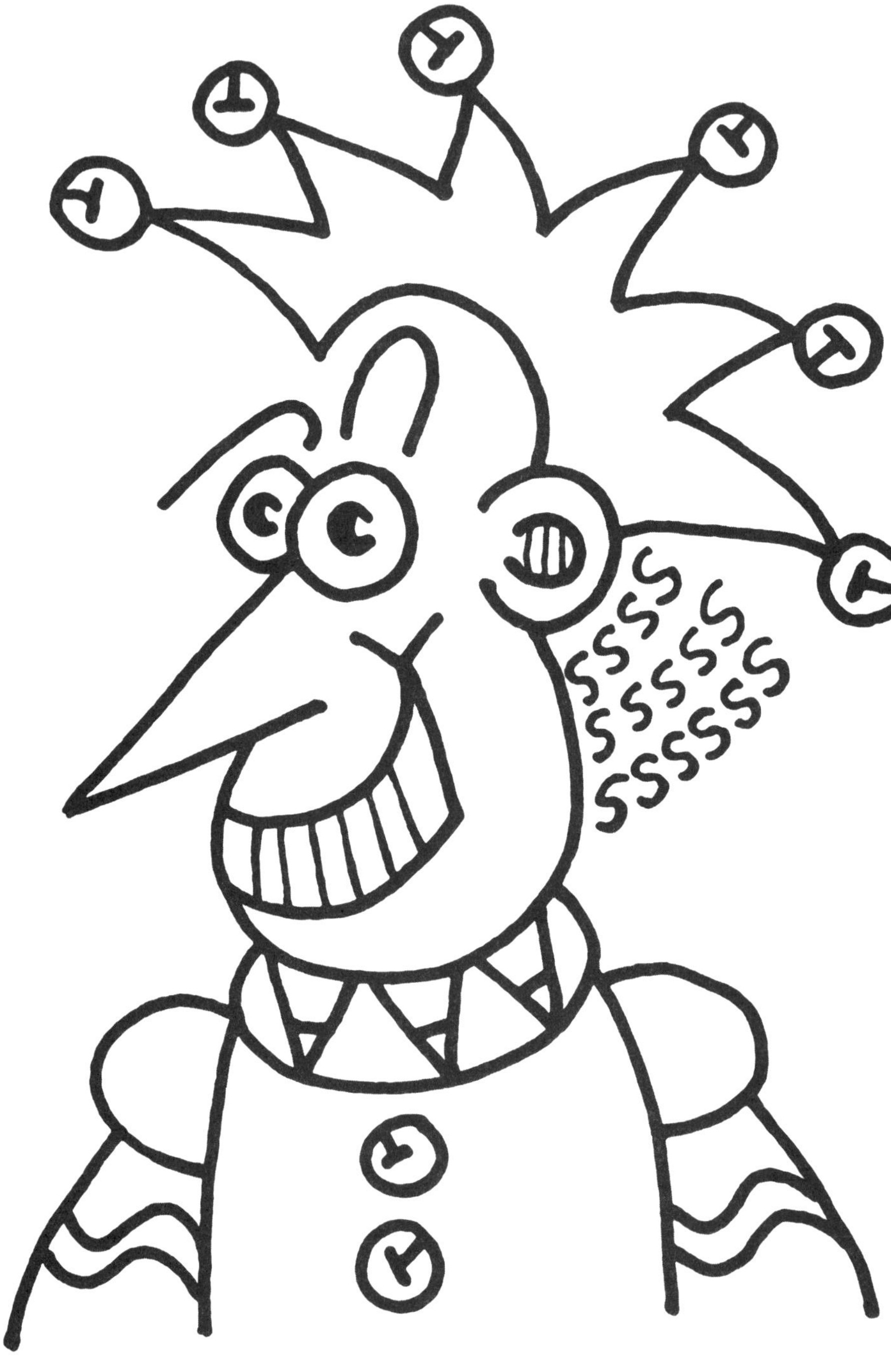

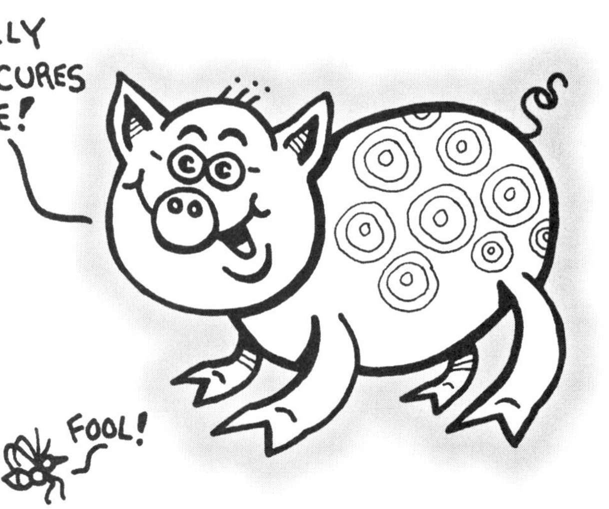

This JESTER is a favorite at WAVY COURT, where he constantly keeps the royal family smiling. Whenever they hear his bells jingling, they know that major league laughs are coming their way.

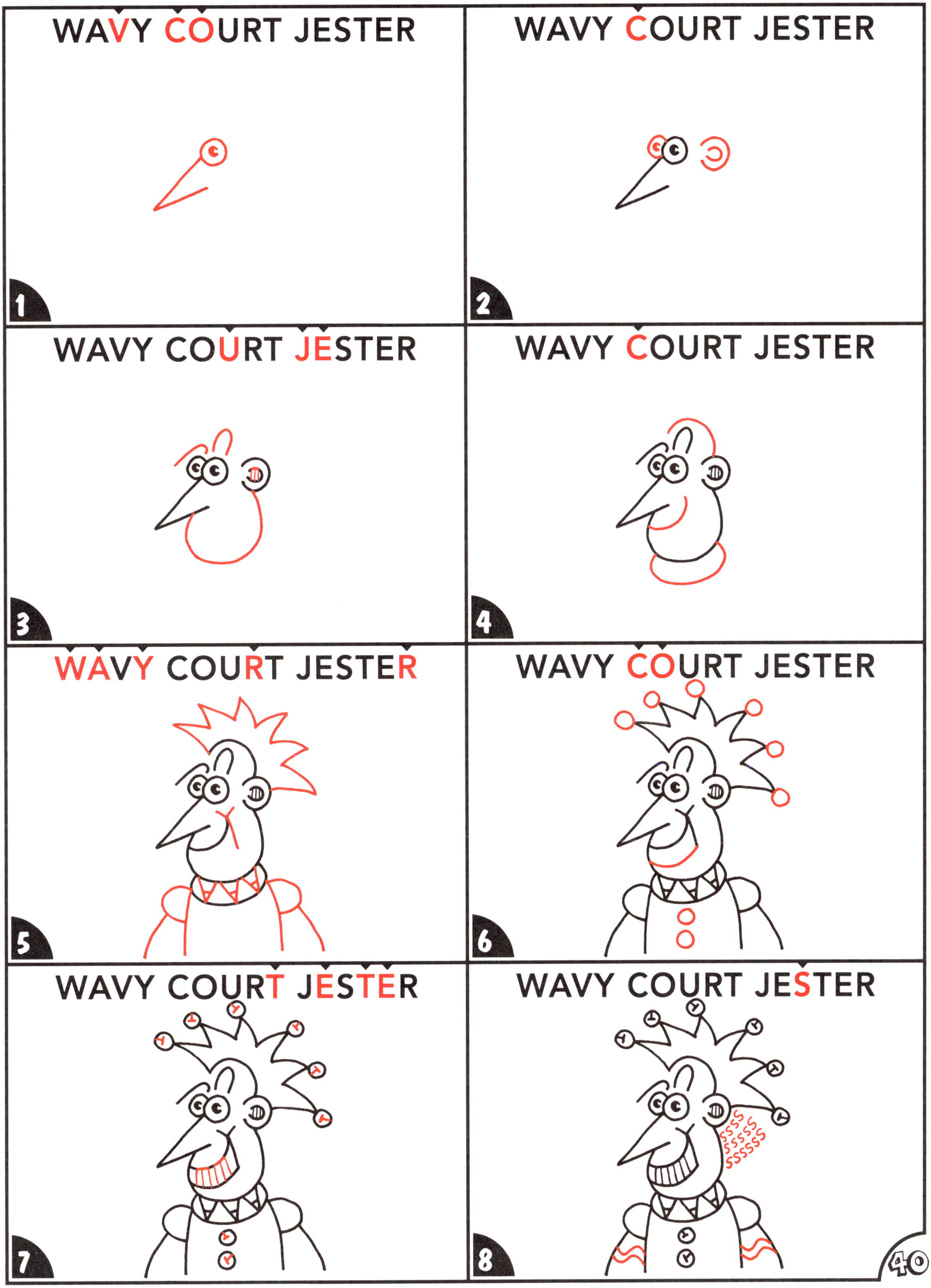
WAVY COURT JESTER
1
WAVY COURT JESTER
2
WAVY COURT JESTER
3
WAVY COURT JESTER
4
WAVY COURT JESTER
5
WAVY COURT JESTER
6
WAVY COURT JESTER
7
WAVY COURT JESTER
8

THE ONE CUTE GiRL PRiNCESS

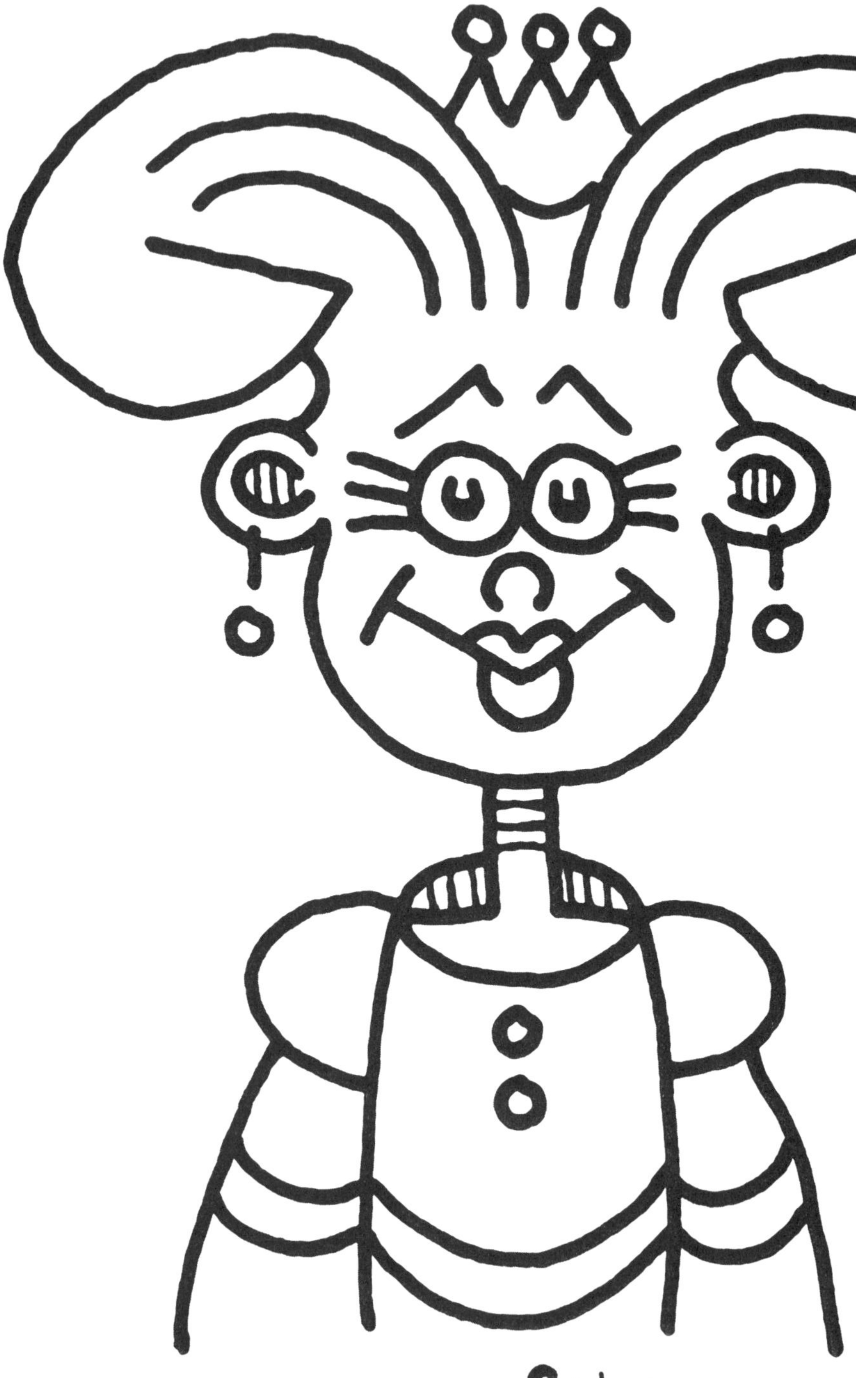

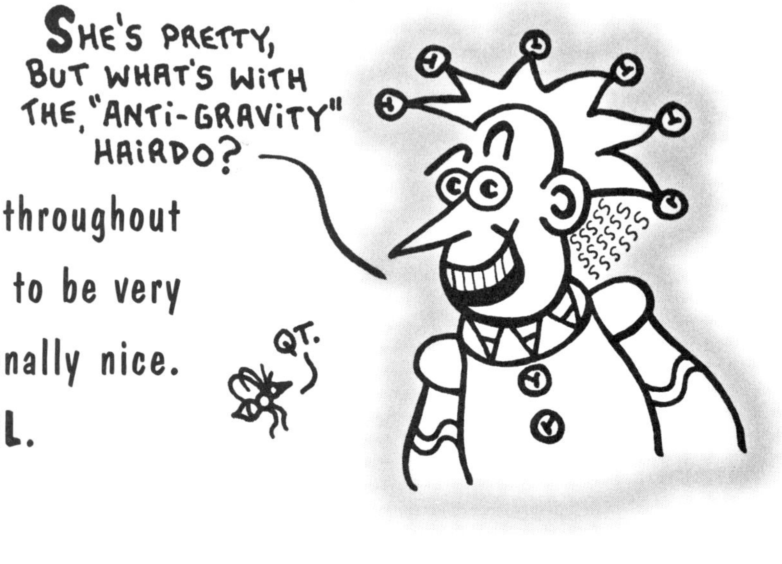

The princess of Wavy Court is adored throughout the kingdom. Her subjects consider her to be very kind, extremely generous, and exceptionally nice. On top of it all, she's **ONE CUTE GiRL**.

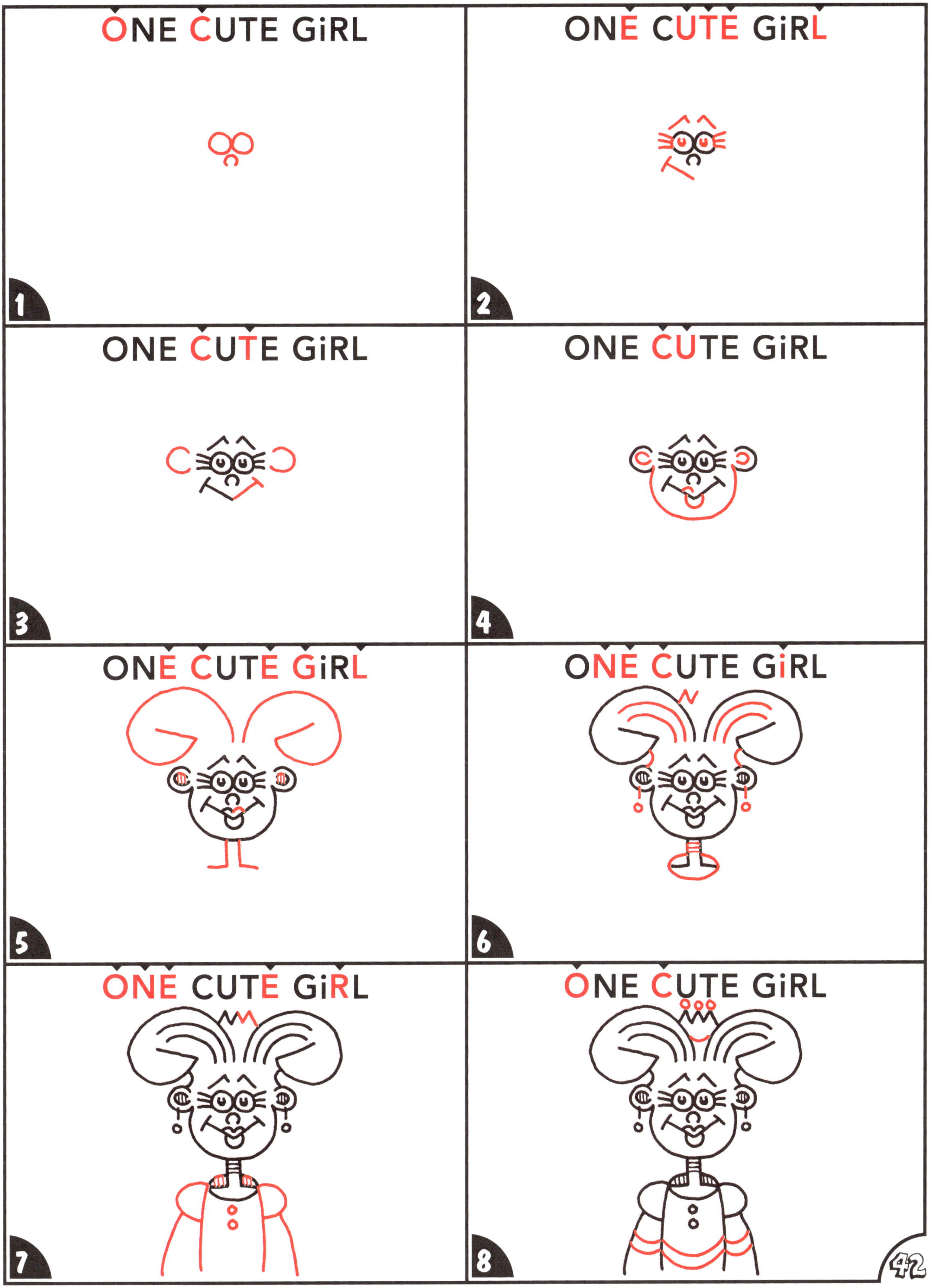
ONE CUTE GiRL
1
ONE CUTE GiRL
2
ONE CUTE GiRL
3
ONE CUTE GiRL
4
ONE CUTE GiRL
5
ONE CUTE GiRL
6
ONE CUTE GiRL
7
ONE CUTE GiRL
8

THE MOUSE VOiCE MOUSE

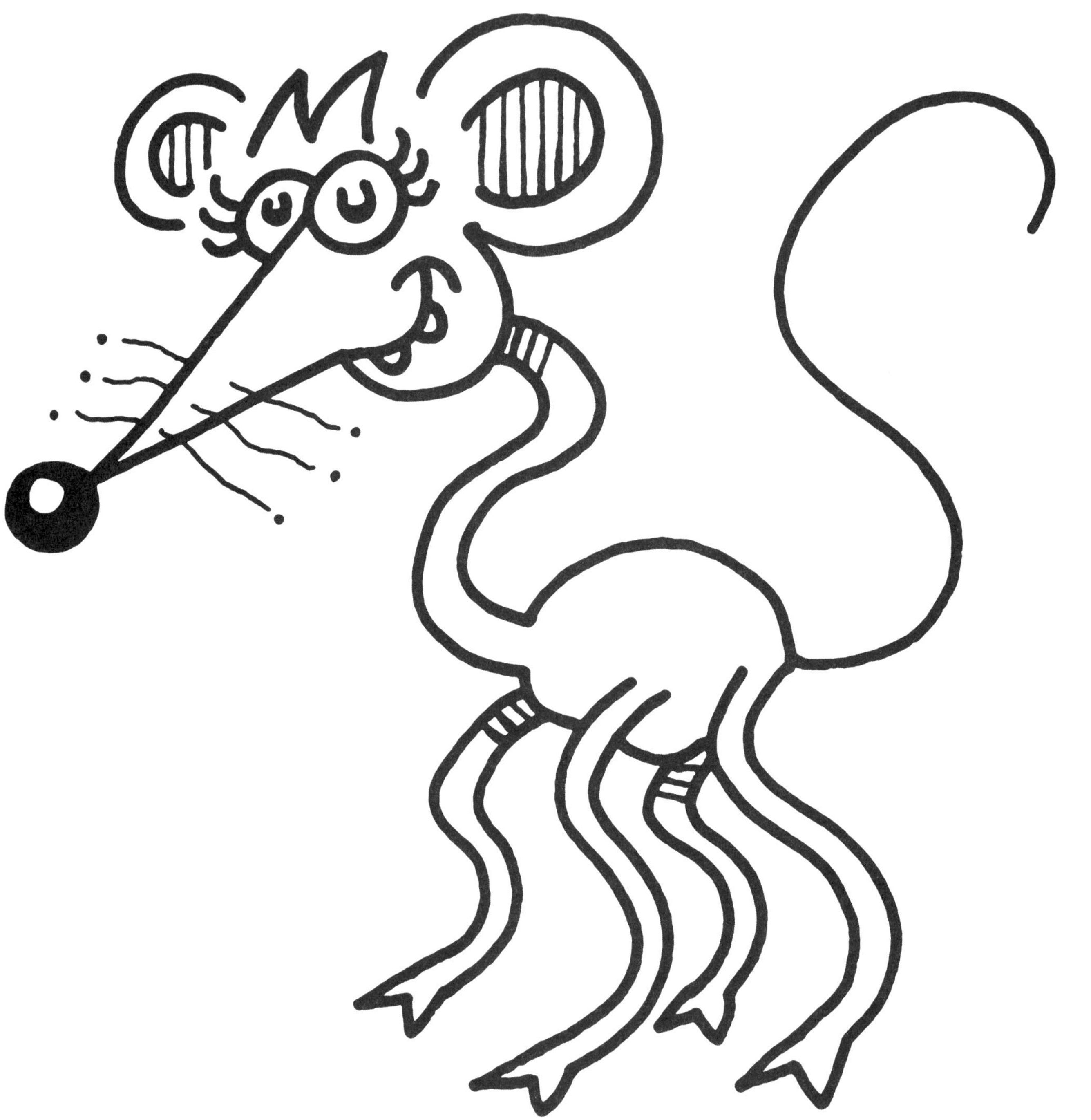

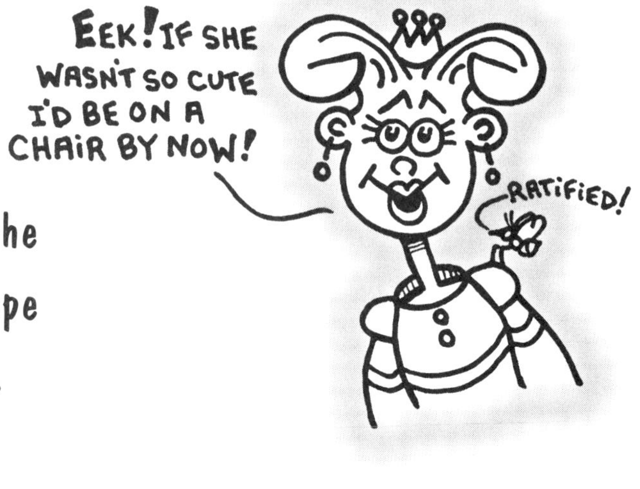

That high-pitched squeaking sound behind the fridge could only be a **MOUSE VOiCE**. Let's hope it's not of the long-necked, long-legged variety.

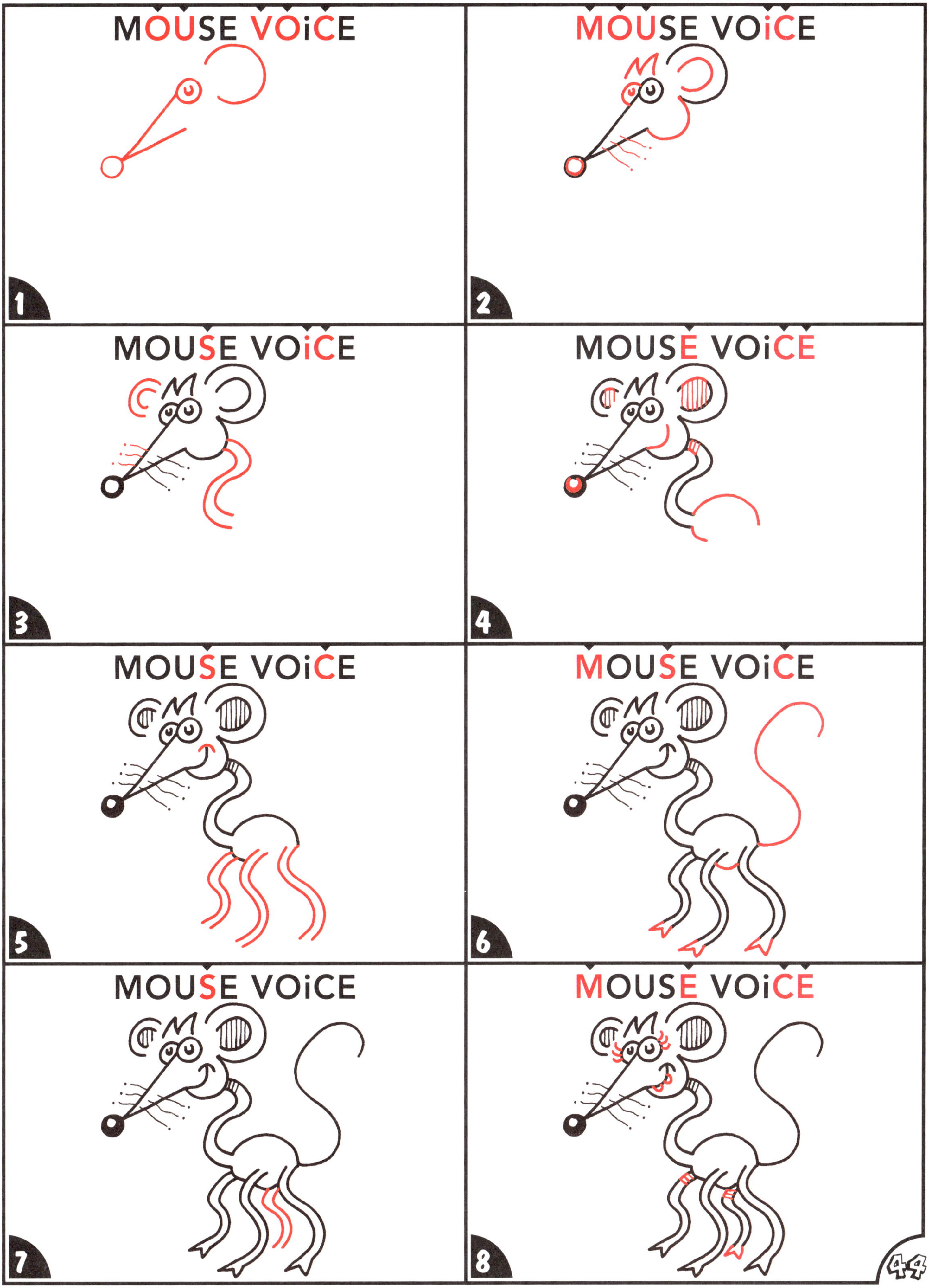
MOUSE VOiCE
1
MOUSE VOiCE
2
MOUSE VOiCE
3
MOUSE VOiCE
4
MOUSE VOiCE
5
MOUSE VOiCE
6
MOUSE VOiCE
7
MOUSE VOiCE
8

THE ZOO EEL SHOCK! ELECTRiC EEL

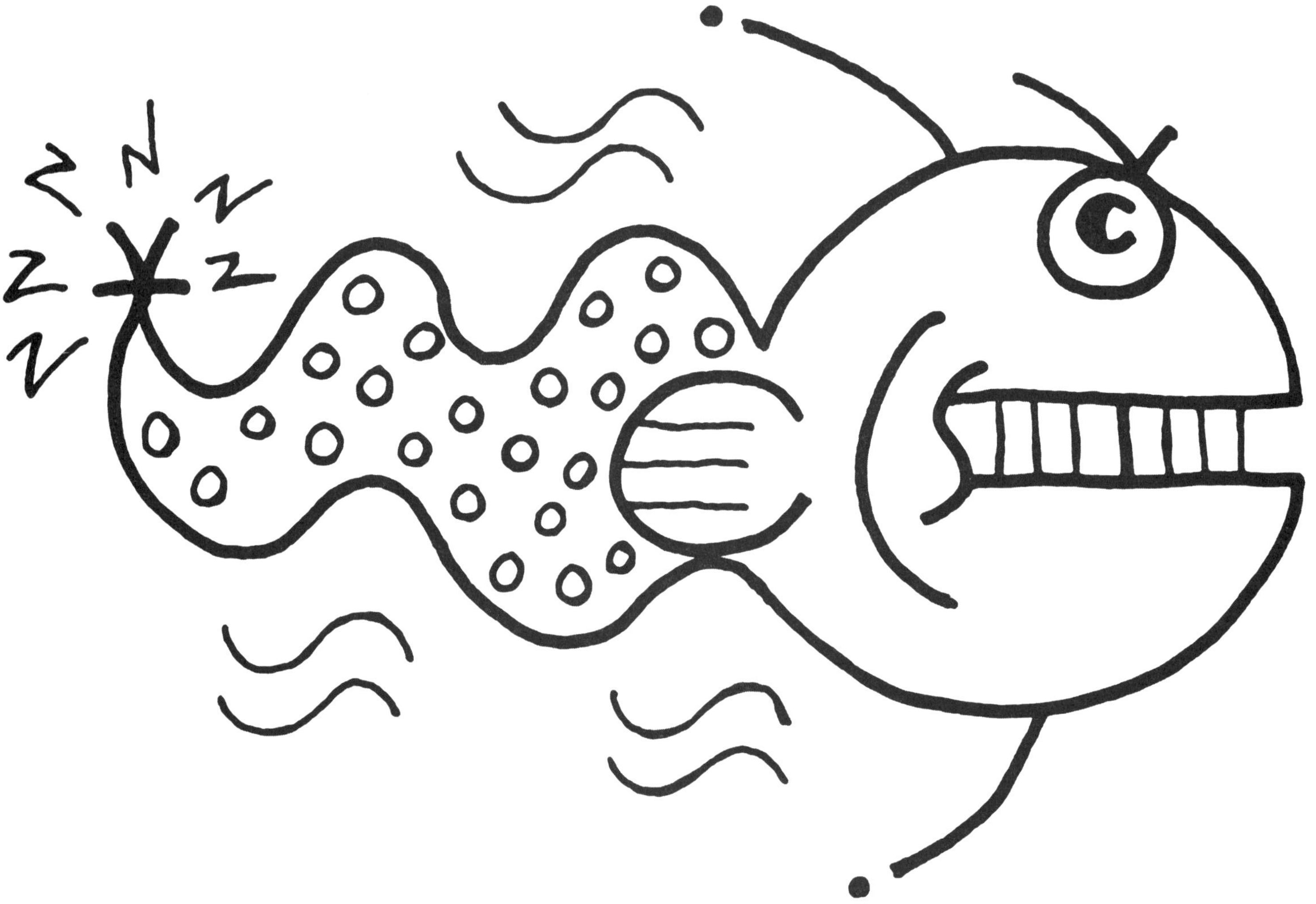

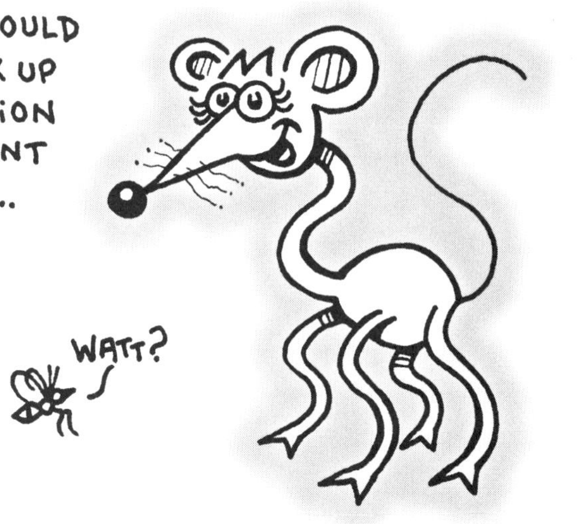

Captured in the wild and housed in a special insulated tank at the **ZOO**, this electric **EEL** packs a high voltage **SHOCK!** in its spiky electrode.

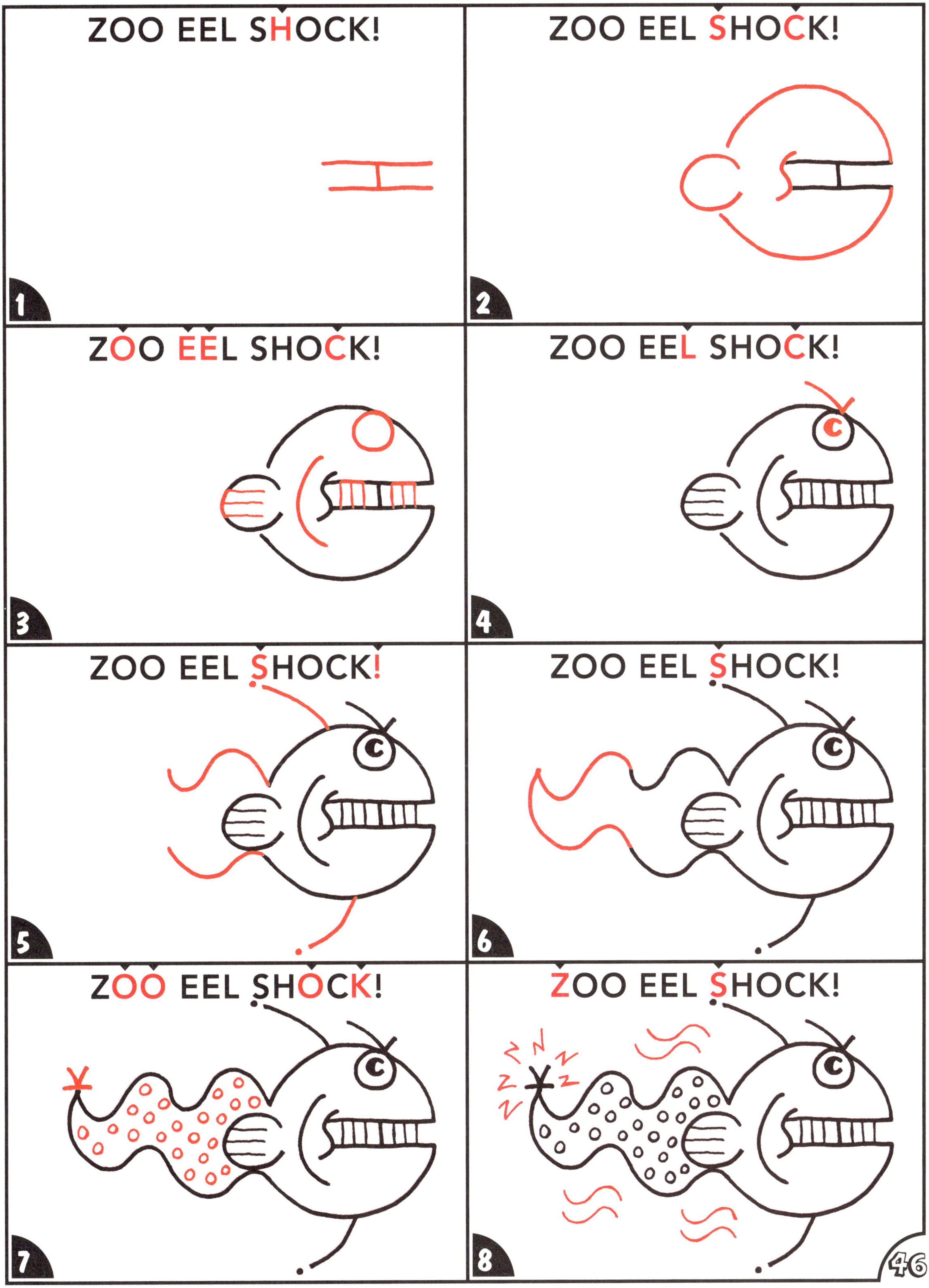
ZOO EEL SHOCK!
1
ZOO EEL SHOCK!
2
ZOO EEL SHOCK!
3
ZOO EEL SHOCK!
4
ZOO EEL SHOCK!
5
ZOO EEL SHOCK!
6
ZOO EEL SHOCK!
7
ZOO EEL SHOCK!
8

THE PiRATE'S CAVE PiRATE

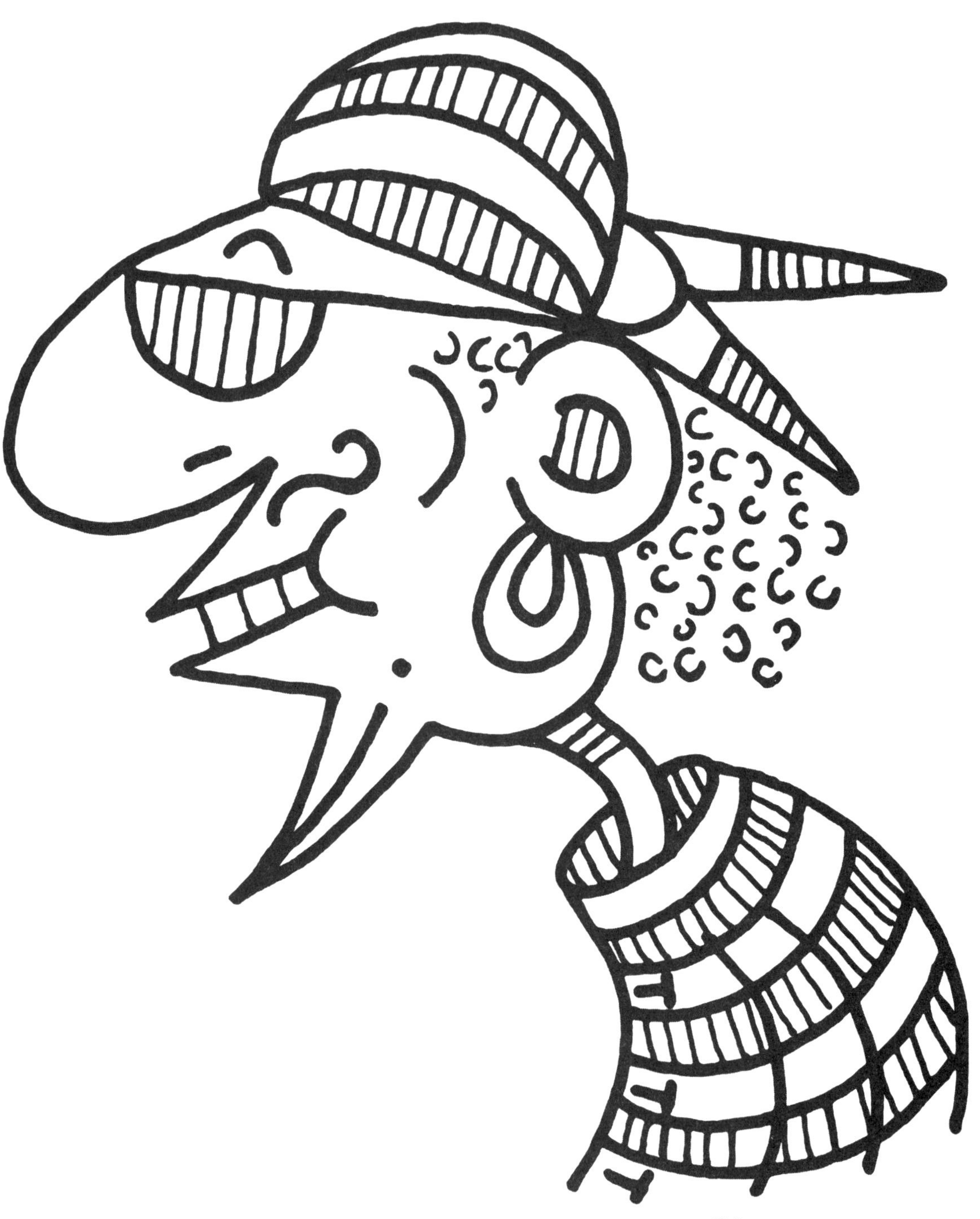

When not wreaking havoc on the high seas, this **PiRATE** hides out in a secret **CAVE**. Concealed there, he washes his bandana, curls his mustache, and irons his eye patch.

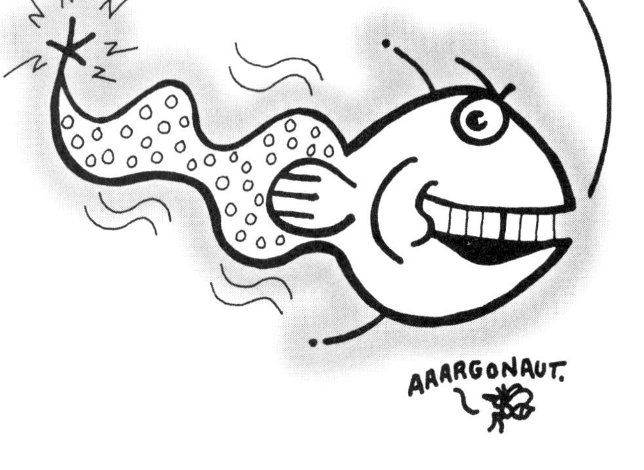

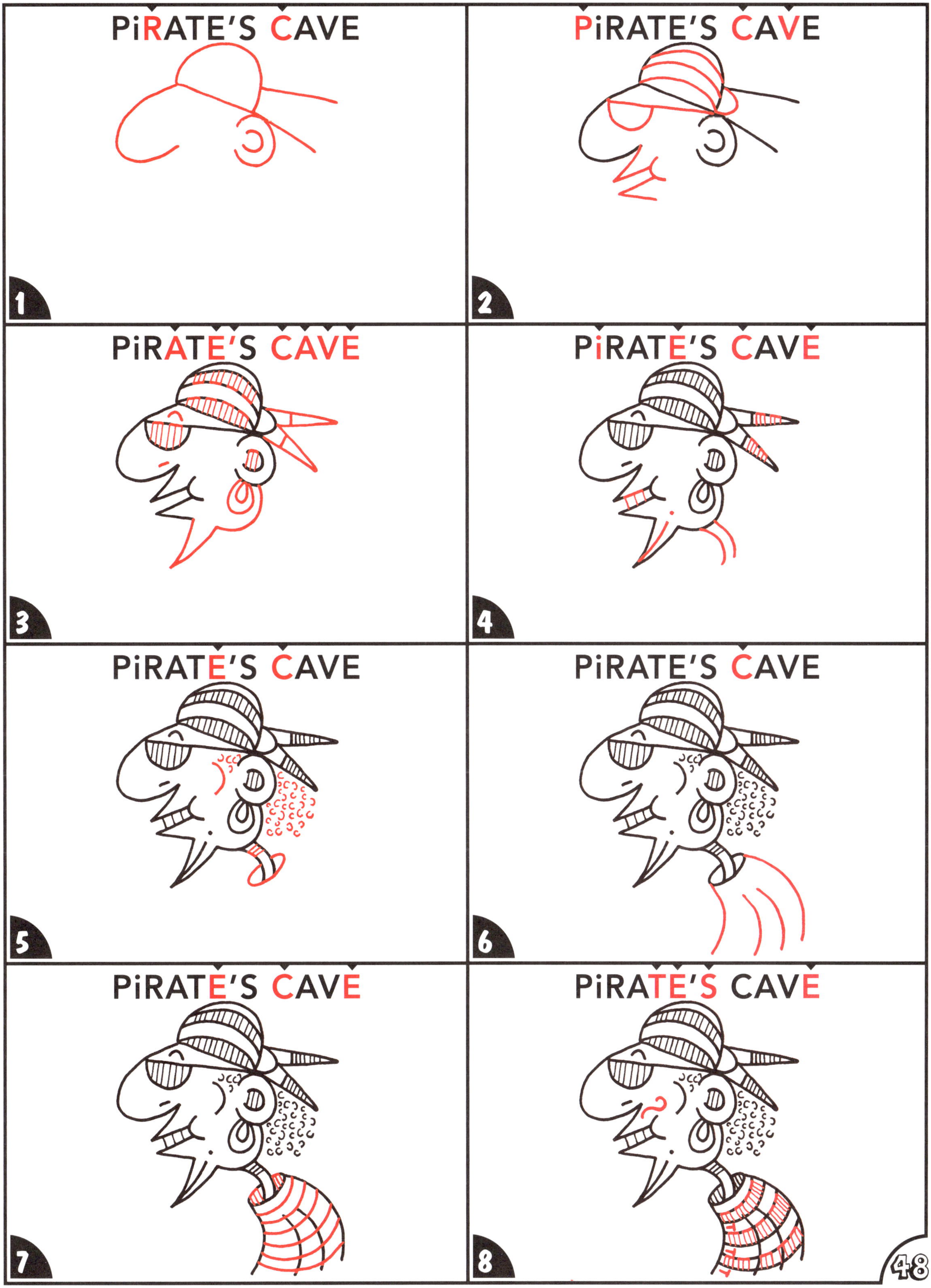
PiRATE'S CAVE
1
PiRATE'S CAVE
2
PiRATE'S CAVE
3
PiRATE'S CAVE
4
PiRATE'S CAVE
5
PiRATE'S CAVE
6
PiRATE'S CAVE
7
PiRATE'S CAVE
8

THE EXTRA QUiCK DUCKLiNG

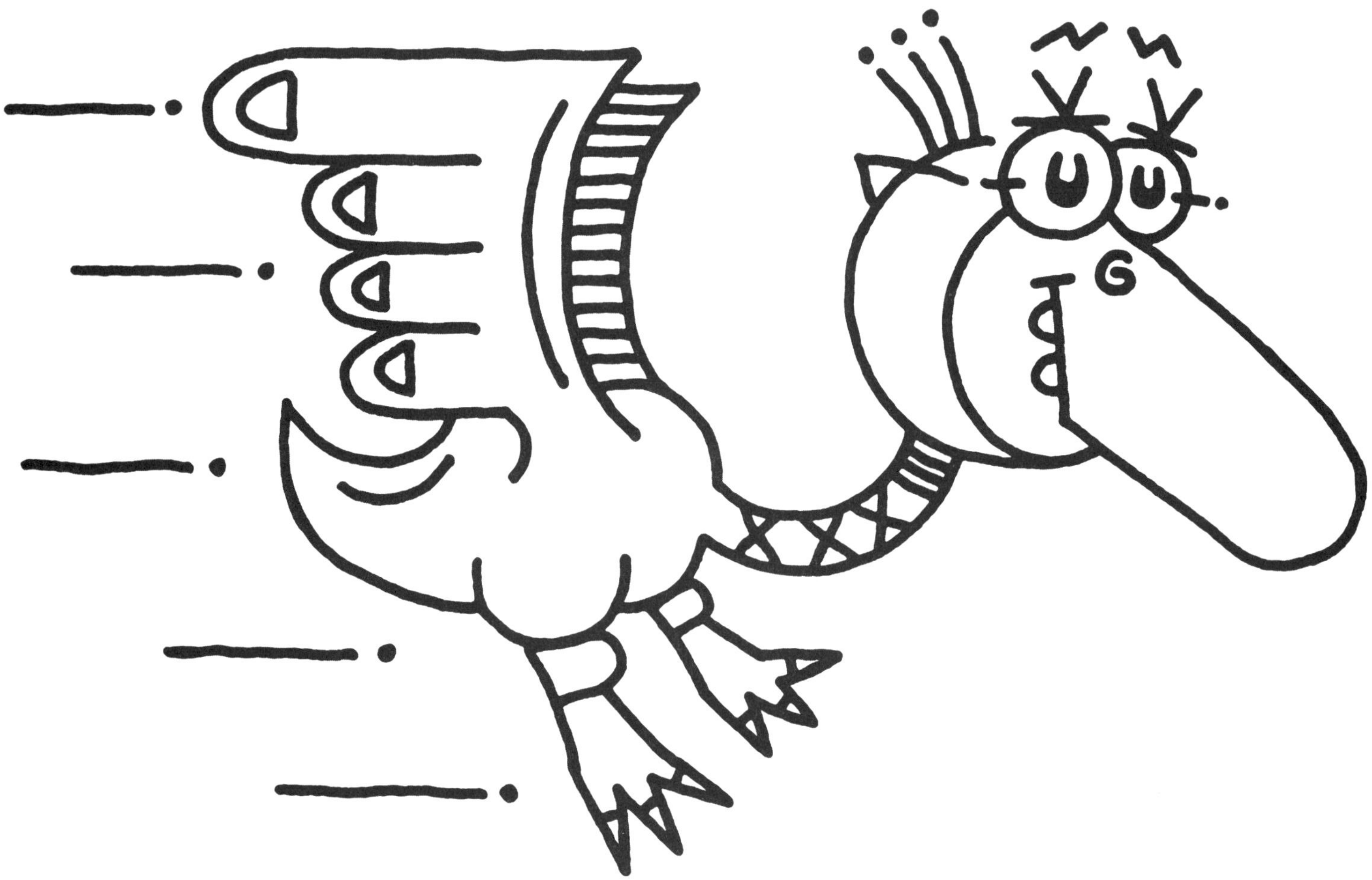

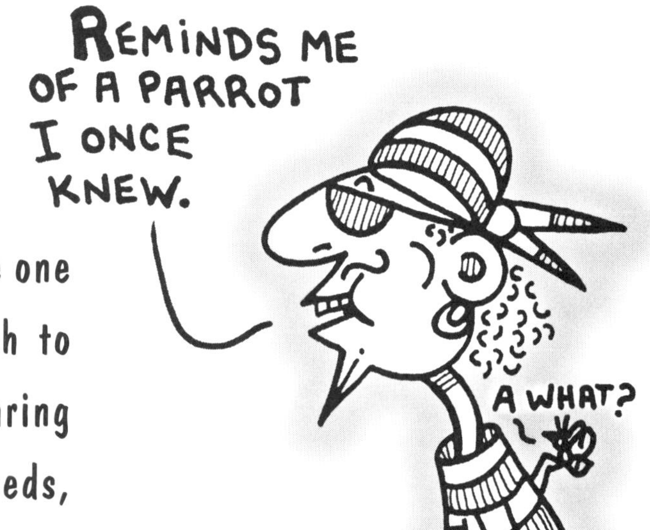

The mother duck knew from early on that the one constantly moving egg in her nest would hatch to become an **EXTRA QUiCK DUCKLiNG**. Wearing safety glasses for protection at high flying speeds, this young bird is destined to lead the flock formations.

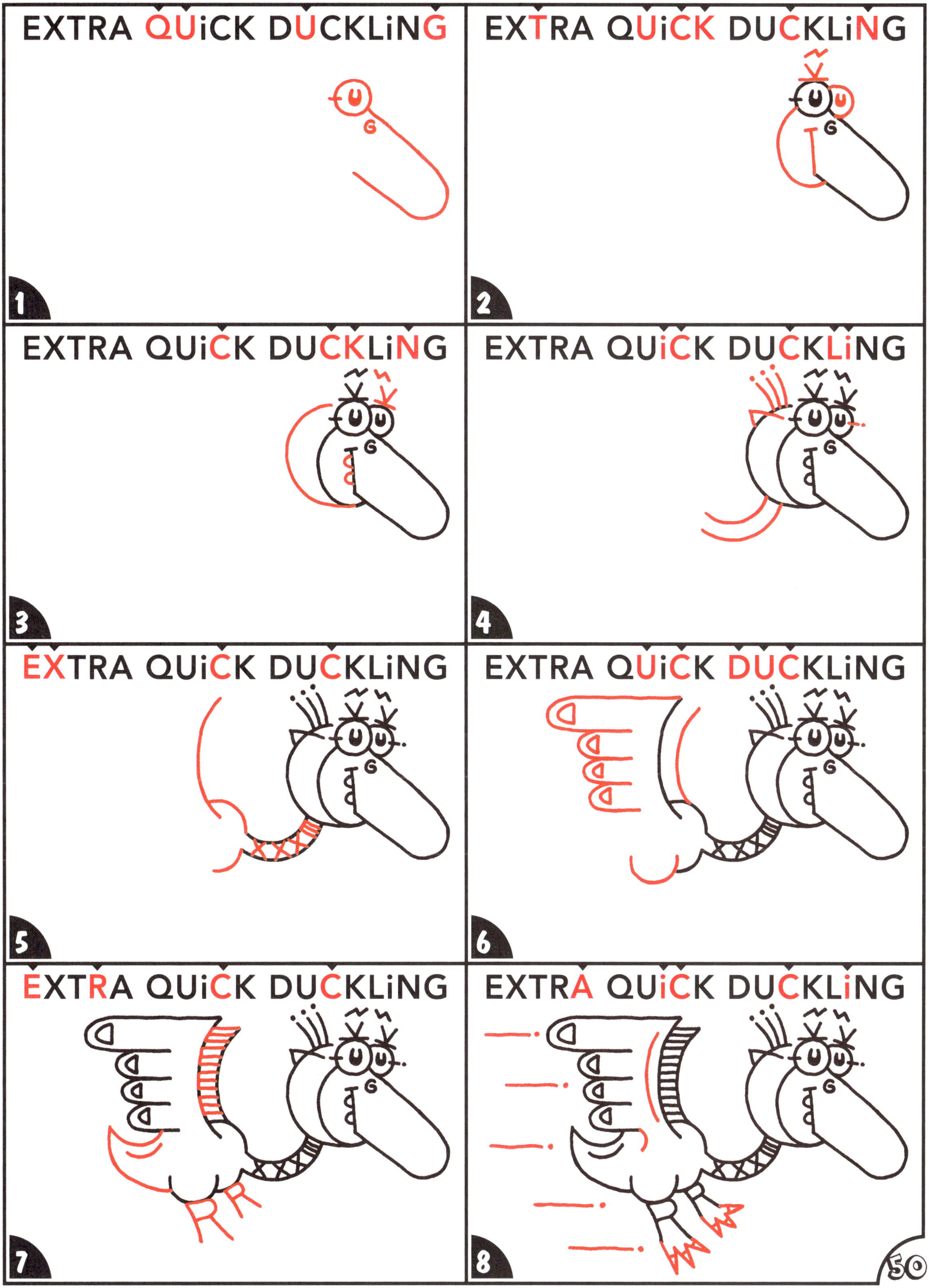
EXTRA QUiCK DUCKLiNG
1
EXTRA QUiCK DUCKLiNG
2
EXTRA QUiCK DUCKLiNG
3
EXTRA QUiCK DUCKLiNG
4
EXTRA QUiCK DUCKLiNG
5
EXTRA QUiCK DUCKLiNG
6
EXTRA QUiCK DUCKLiNG
7
EXTRA QUiCK DUCKLiNG
8

THE **ACTiVATE!** ALiEN

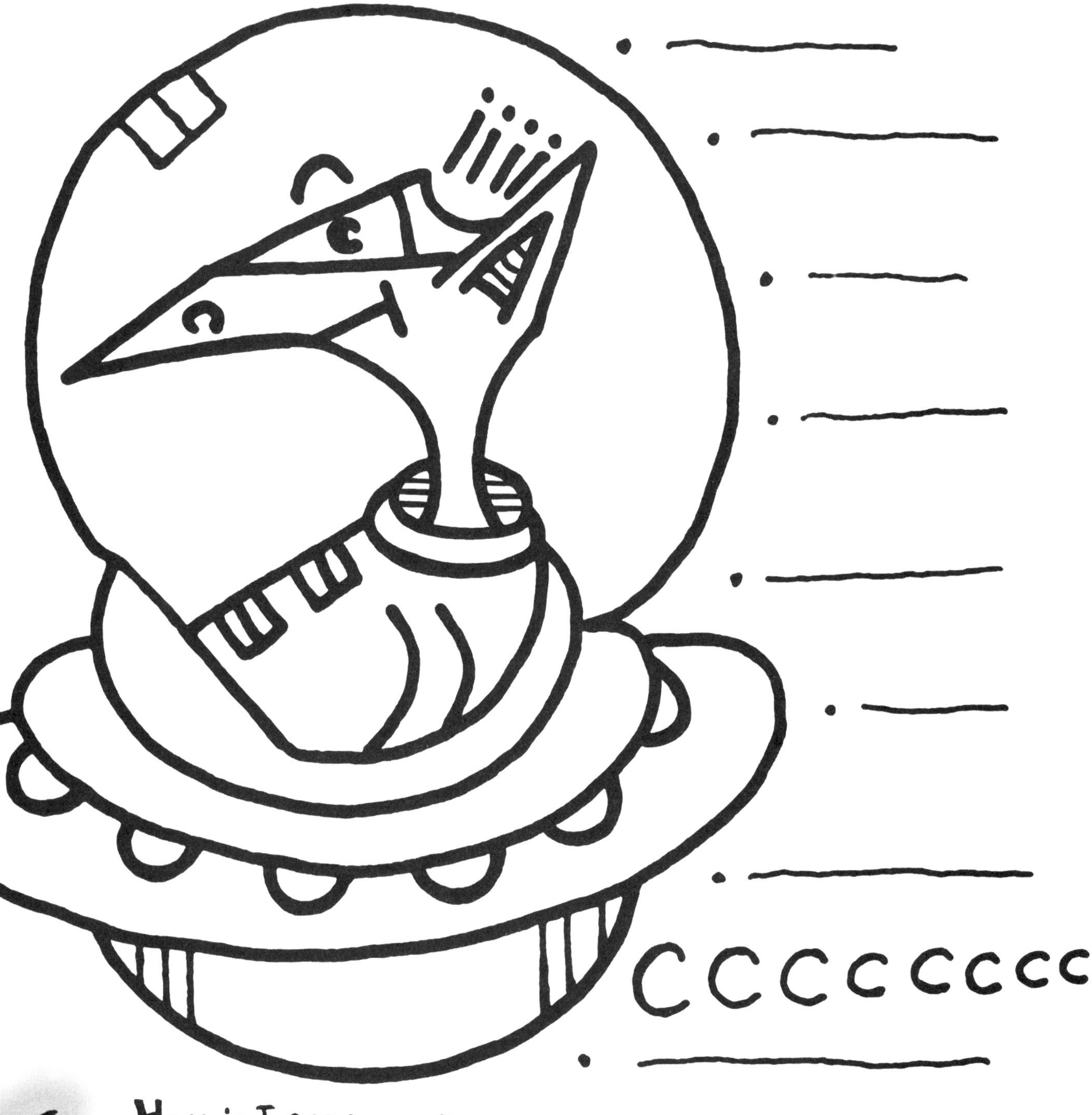

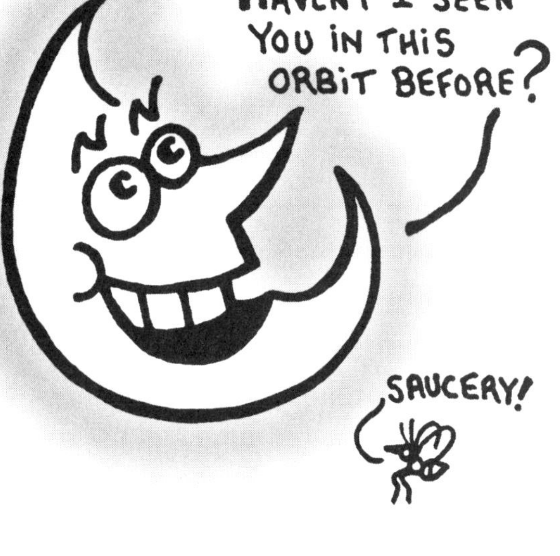

Cruising at just over light speed, this alien roams the galaxy, issuing commands to his robotic flying saucer such as, "**ACTiVATE!** the landing sequence!," or "**ACTiVATE!** the meteor defense shield!," or sometimes, "**ACTiVATE!** the microwave oven!"

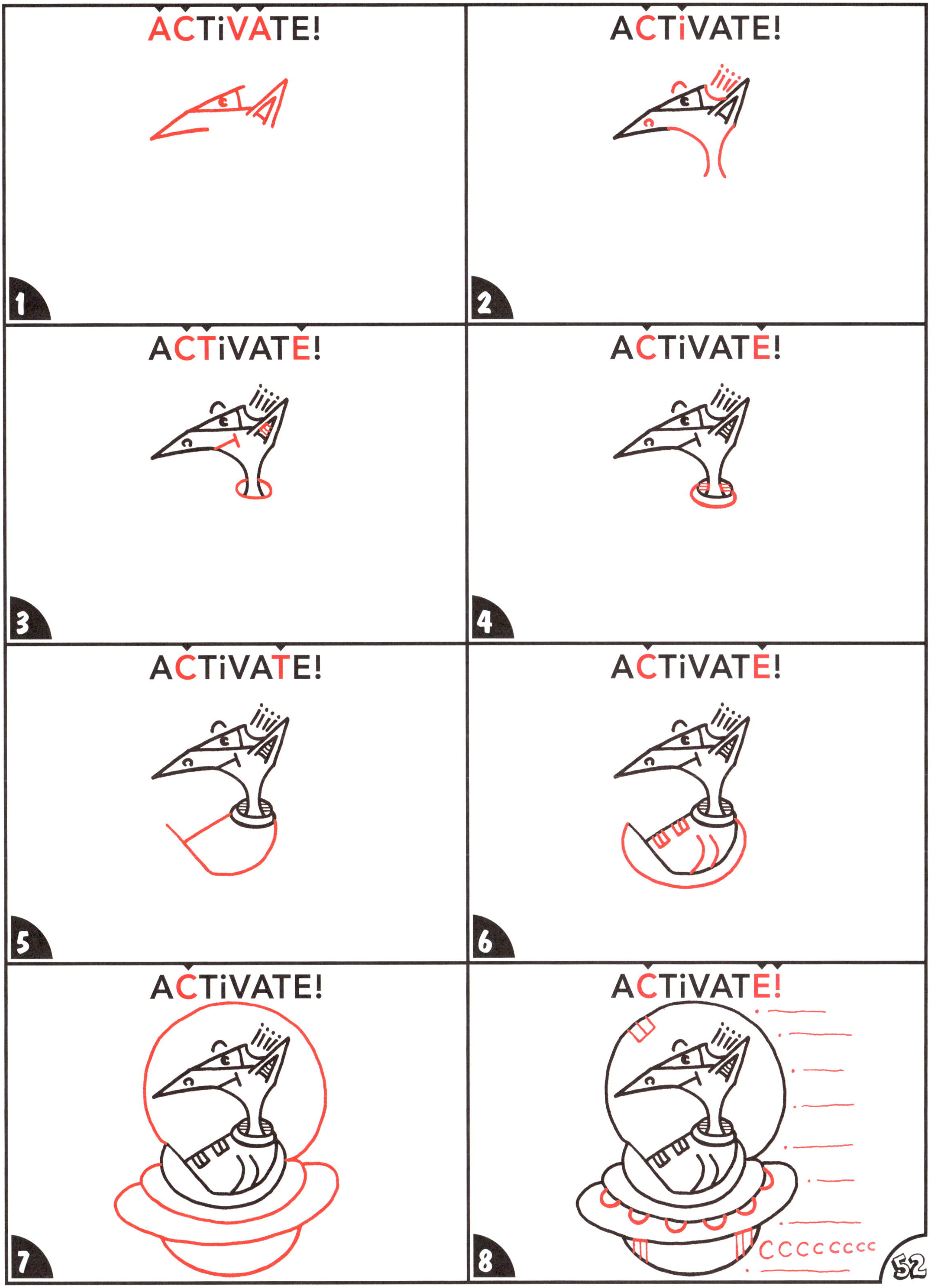
ACTiVATE!
1
ACTiVATE!
2
ACTiVATE!
3
ACTiVATE!
4
ACTiVATE!
5
ACTiVATE!
6
ACTiVATE!
7
ACTiVATE!
CCCCCCCC
8

THE AUTHOR

In 1984, as a recent graduate of Dartmouth College, Steve Brosnihan was inspired and encouraged by fellow alumnus Theodor Seuss Geisel to pursue a career as a cartoonist. Back in his native Rhode Island, Steve received further encouragement from popular cartoonist Don Bousquet, whose work Steve had long admired. In the years since, Steve has been creating cartoons for local, regional and national publications.

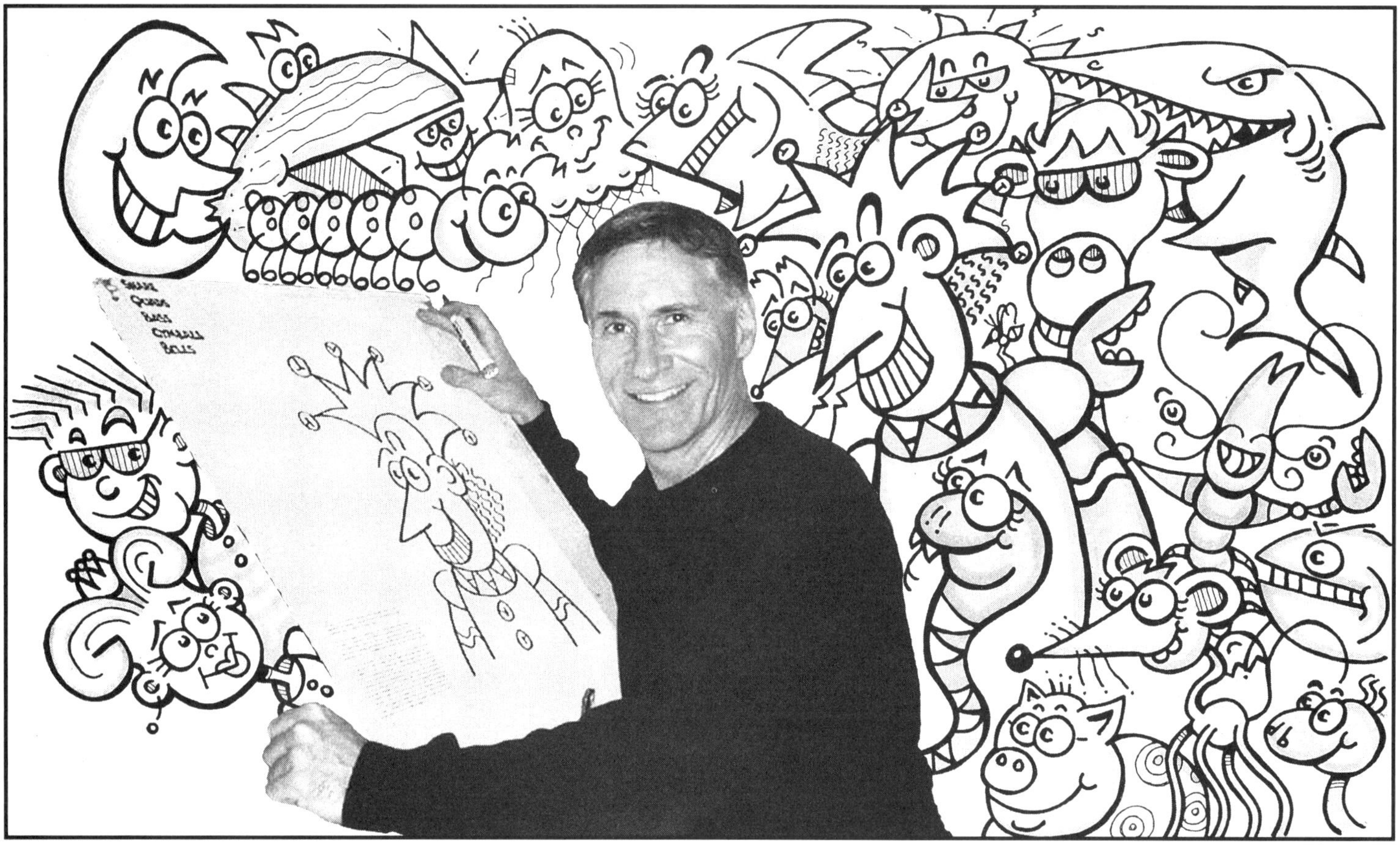

While working at bedside with hospitalized children, Steve developed his Cartoonagrams™ method as a means to bring lasting smiles and skills to his students. Steve continues to teach Cartoonagrams™ to people of all ages, in settings which include hospitals, schools, camps, libraries, and senior centers.

Since 1991 Steve has been the resident cartoonist at Hasbro Children's Hospital in Providence, RI. He is also a volunteer counselor and "Cartoon Guru" at The Hole in the Wall Gang Camp for children in Ashford, CT.

Arrangements to book Steve for a live Cartoonagrams™ group teaching session can be made by emailing him at steve@cartoonagrams.com. Further information is available at www.cartoonagrams.com.

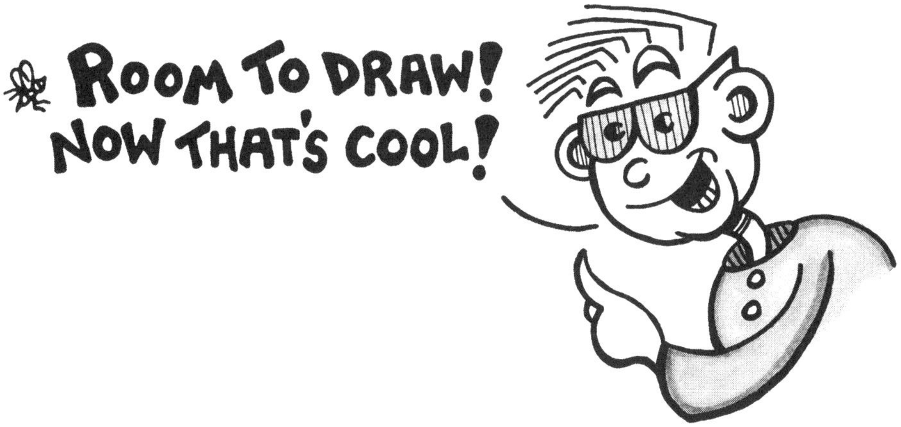
ROOM TO DRAW!
NOW THAT'S COOL!

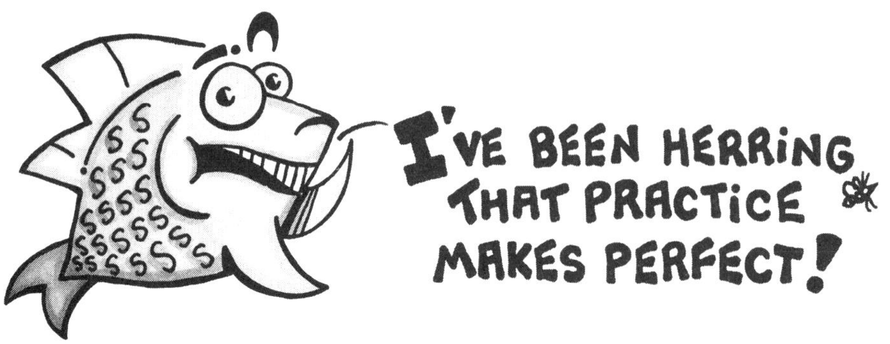
I'VE BEEN HERRING THAT PRACTICE MAKES PERFECT!

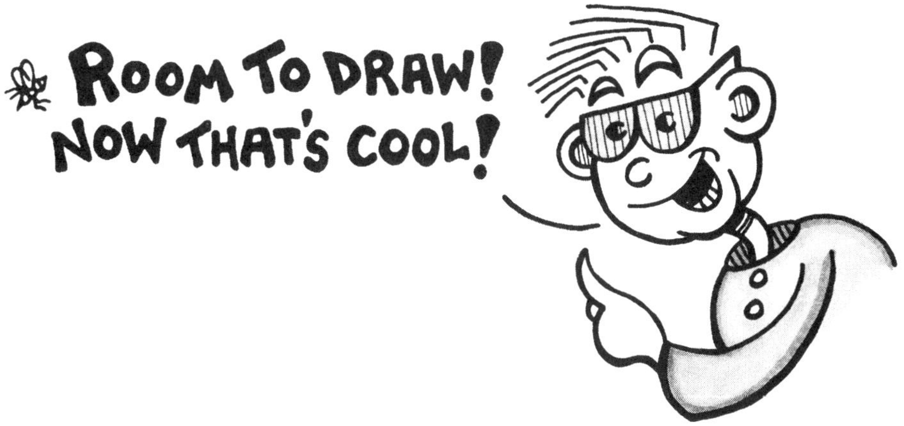
ROOM TO DRAW!
NOW THAT'S COOL!

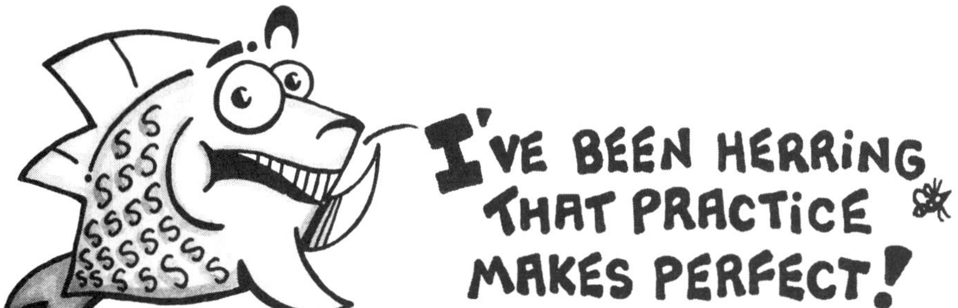
I'VE BEEN HERRING
THAT PRACTICE
MAKES PERFECT!

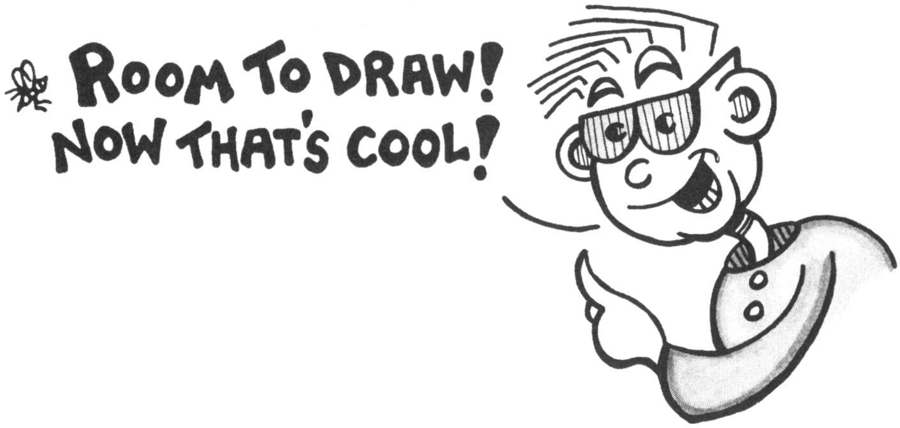
ROOM TO DRAW! NOW THAT'S COOL!

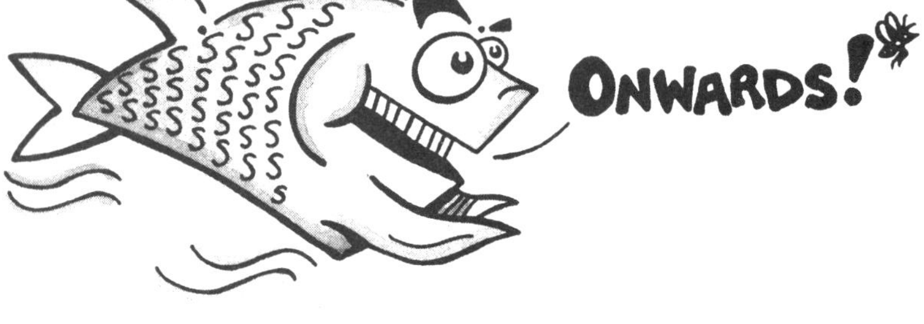
ONWARDS!